Heroes and Villains Entertainment
presents

EPOCH™

published by
Top Cow Productions, Inc.
Los Angeles

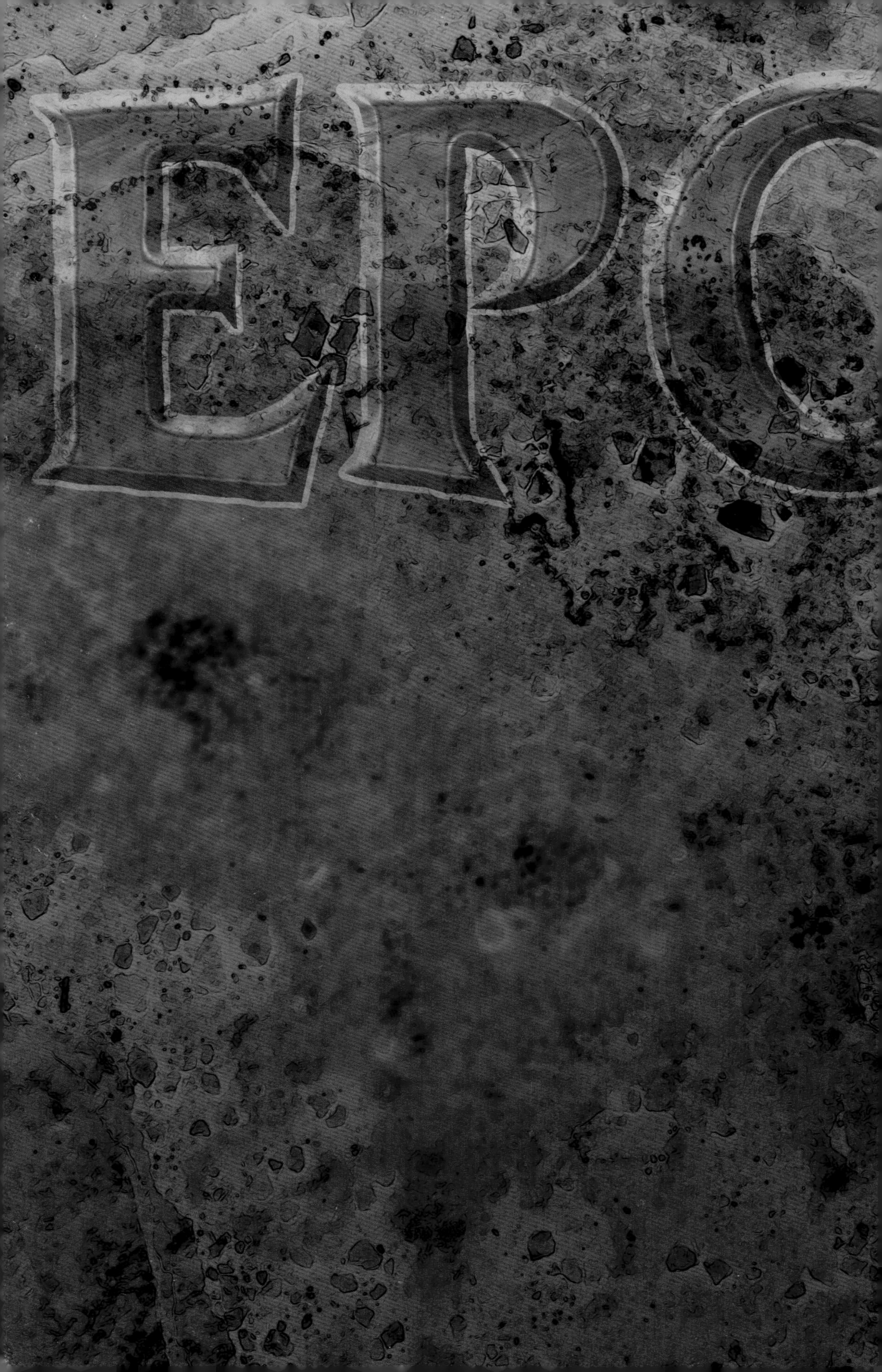

VOLUME 1

Written by
KEVIN McCARTHY
Art by
PAOLO PANTALENA

Colors by
Bill Farmer
with Jorge Fares

Letters by
Troy Peteri

For this eddition cover art by:
Paolo Pantalena & Paolo Barbieri

Logo Design by:
Phil Smith

Original editions edited by:
Filip Sablik

For this edition book design and layout by:
Jana Cook

FOR TOP COW PRODUCTIONS, INC.
Marc Silvestri - CEO
Matt Hawkins - President & COO
Bryan Rountree - Managing Editor
Elena Salcedo - Operations Manager
Besty Gonia - Production Assistant

For Heroes and Villains Entertainment:
Markus Goerg
Dick Hillenbrand
Mikhail Nayfeld

For rights inquiries contact Heroes and Villains Entertainment:
323.850.2990
info@heroesandvillains-ent.com

IMAGE COMICS, INC.
Robert Kirkman - chief operating officer
Erik Larsen - chief financial officer
Todd McFarlane - president
Marc Silvestri - chief executive officer
Jim Valentino - vice-president

Eric Stephenson - publisher
Todd Martinez - sales & licensing coordinator
Jennifer de Guzman - pr & marketing director
Branwyn Bigglestone - accounts manager
Emily Miller - administrative assistant
Jamie Parreno - marketing assistant
Sarah deLaine - events coordinator
Kevin Yuen - digital rights coordinator
Jonathan Chan - production manager
Drew Gill - art director
Monica Garcia - production artist
Vincent Kukua - production artist
Jana Cook - production artist
www.imagecomics.com

EPOCH
FIRST PRINTING. $19.99 USD
ISBN: 978-1-60706-587-6
Published by Image Comics, Inc. Office of publication: 2134 Allston Way, Second Floor, Berkeley, CA 94704. Originally published in single magazine form as EPOCH #1-5.

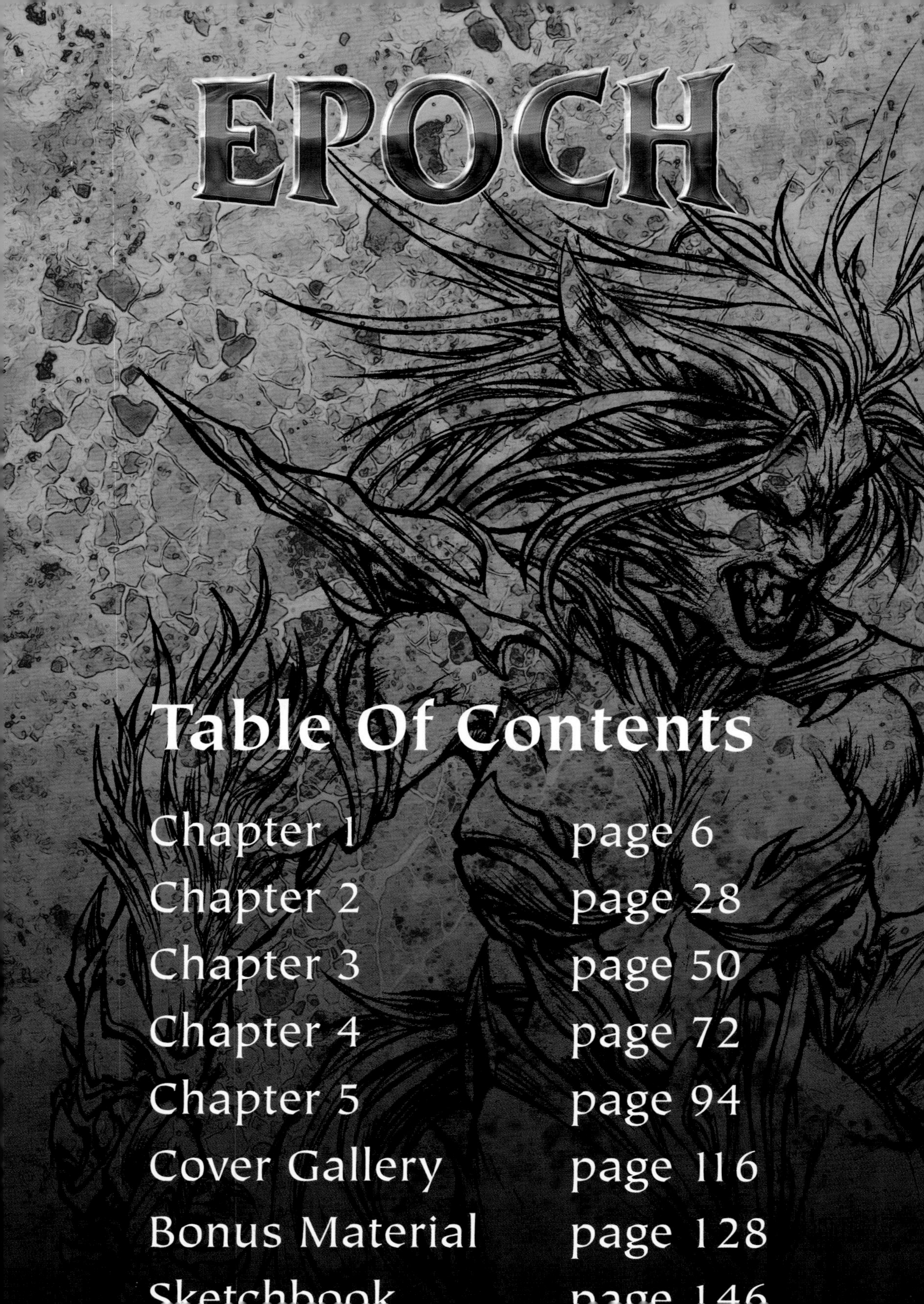

EPOCH

Table Of Contents

Chapter 1 page 6
Chapter 2 page 28
Chapter 3 page 50
Chapter 4 page 72
Chapter 5 page 94
Cover Gallery page 116
Bonus Material page 128
Sketchbook page 146

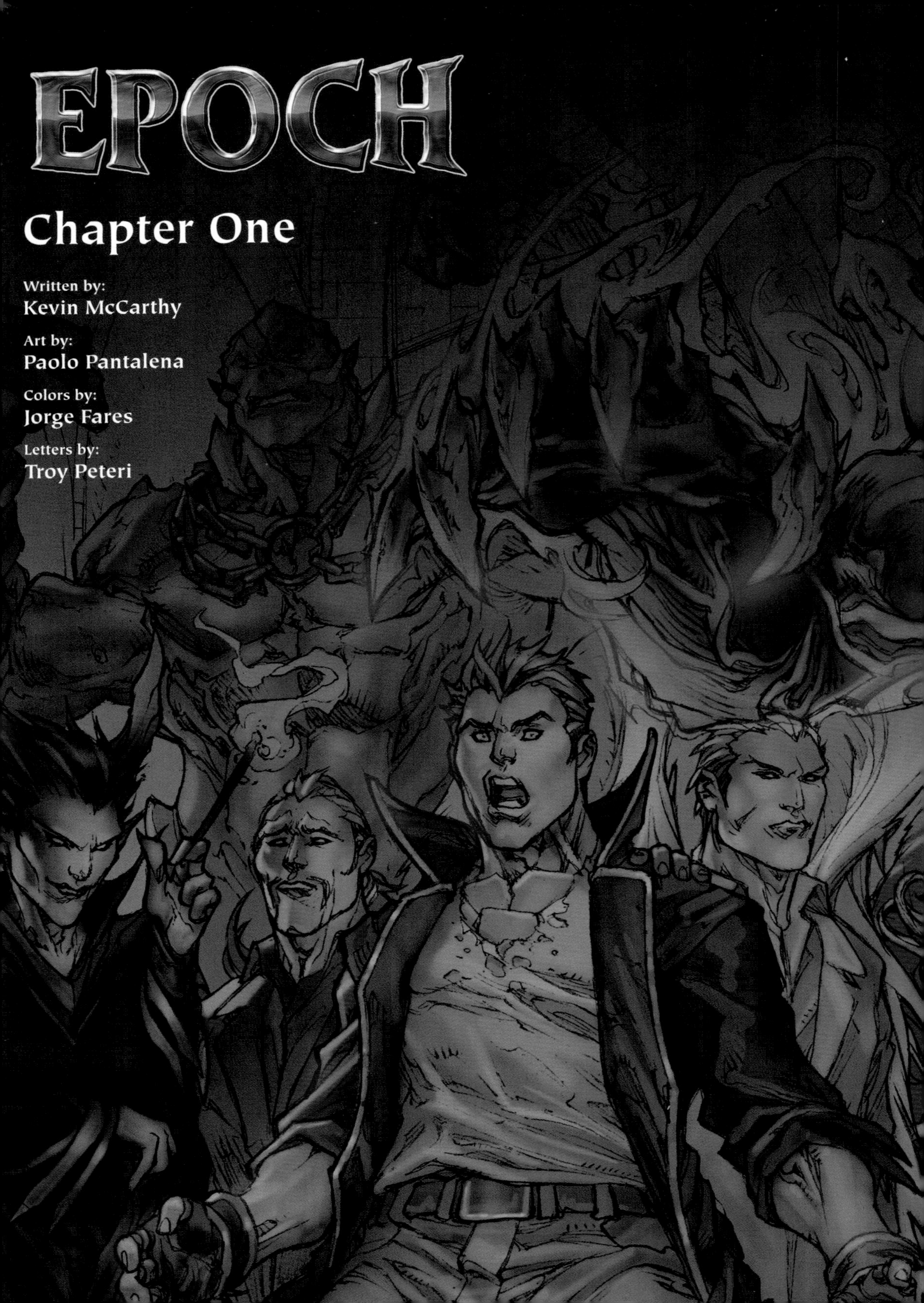
EPOCH
Chapter One
Written by:
Kevin McCarthy
Art by:
Paolo Pantalena
Colors by:
Jorge Fares
Letters by:
Troy Peteri

I was always kind of a nervous kid. Nightmares. Something under the bed. I remember my father telling me there was nothing to be afraid of. That there's no such thing as MONSTERS.
I believed him then. But now I know better.
After ten years on the force, I've seen enough PROOF that they exist.
REAL monsters don't hide in our closets or under the bed. They're all AROUND us. Living normal lives. Pretending.
You can't always TELL a monster by its appearance. The REALLY dangerous ones look just like everybody else. They're our friends and neighbors.
And we usually don't learn the TRUTH about them until it's already too late.

WEEKS EARLIER, 18TH PRECINCT MIDTOWN NORTH, NYC.
My partner and I have been working a series of murders. So far, our only lead is an ATM video of a car leaving the latest crime scene-- registered to U.S.Congresswoman MYA TOKAGE.
DETECTIVE WRIGHT'S GOT A WHALE OF A WITNESS IN THE BOX. WHY ISN'T MICHAEL WITH HIM, LIEUTENANT? THOUGHT HE WAS THE PRIMARY...
GOT HELD UP FOLLOWING ANOTHER LEAD DOWNTOWN. TOO BAD. I COULD USE HIM IN THERE...HIS PARTNER'S OFF HIS GAME TONIGHT.
She agrees to come in and answer some questions as long as there are no TV news crews waiting for her when she gets here. Smart lady.
Been sweating her almost four hours. She hasn't asked for a lawyer. Hasn't even asked to use the BATHROOM. A real tough customer.
SECURITY CAMERAS PUT YOU THERE AT AROUND MY VIC'S TIME OF DEATH, CONGRESSWOMAN.
THAT TIME OF NIGHT, IT'S PRETTY QUIET. SOMETHING LIKE THESE PHOTOS GOES DOWN? YOU HAD TO HAVE HEARD IT.
IT LOOKS LIKE HE WAS TORN APART BY A WILD ANIMAL!

AND WHEN THE "ANIMAL" WHO DID THIS HEARS THAT I TOLD YOU ANYTHING, I'M NEXT.
WE CAN PROTECT YOU, BUT YOU HAVE TO GIVE ME A NAME.
SIGH FINE. YOU'VE KEPT ME HERE LONG ENOUGH. I'LL TELL YOU WHAT YOU WANT TO KNOW.
BUT FIRST, I'LL NEED IMMUNITY. IN WRITING.
TAP TAP TAP
"IMMUNITY" SOUNDS LIKE THERE'S EVEN MORE YOU'RE NOT TELLING ME...
She gets her deal, and I get my name. It's a shame Michael isn't here for this, but if I don't move on this intel, my guy's in the wind.
WILFRED GLENDON! POLICE! SEARCH WARRANT!
OPEN HER UP, FELLAS.

That's Glendon on the table. He won't be spilling his guts tonight, somebody beat him to it.
SERGEANT VERELLA, IS THE ROOM SECURE?
CLEARRRRGH!
SCHLRRRRIPPT!
WHAT THE F--?! FREEZE!
JONAH -- GET OUT OF THERE!
MICHAEL?

HUNNF!
SKRUNNNCH
NOOOO!
WHAT HAVE YOU DONE?
THIS CAN'T BE HAPPENING.
THIS? IT'S ONLY THE BEGINNING...
WAIT--!
SKA-RAKSH

SHRRIP

THIS IS RECKLESS. EVEN FOR A DEMON. IF SOMEONE WERE TO SEE US--!
FOR YOU TO GO AGAINST THE COUNCIL LIKE THIS, IT DOESN'T EVEN MAKE SENSE. YOU KNOW I WON'T LET YOU RUIN ALL THE PROGRESS WE'VE MADE.
YOU CALL THIS PROGRESS? WE'RE ALL DYING A SLOW DEATH WHILE YOUR USELESS COUNCIL PRETENDS NOTHING'S WRONG. WELL, I'M FINISHED PLAYING THAT LOSING GAME.
WHAT'S USELESS IS TRYING TO GET THROUGH TO YOU. YOU'LL NEVER UNDERSTAND. I CAN SEE THAT NOW.

YOU *WANTED* ME TO VIOLATE MY OWN RULES AND DRAW ME OUT INTO OPEN COMBAT. WELL, YOU'VE *GOT* IT. LET'S *FINISH* THIS.

YOU COULDN'T BEAT ME ALL THOSE YEARS AGO, *DEMON*. AND YOU *STILL* AREN'T UP TO THE TASK...

HUNH? WHUZZAT?!

EVERYTHING'S GOING ACCORDING TO PLAN.

A MAN BURNING *BLUE*.

ROOSEVELT HOSPITAL, 10TH AVENUE AND 59TH STREET, NYC.

Soon as I'm able to hold a pen, the bosses got me filling out paperwork for whatever the hell happened last night.

A lot of good police died, I know that. Why I'm not one of them I really have no clue.

JESUS, JONAH. YOU LOOK LIKE HELL.
YOU SHOULD SEE THE OTHER GUY, POP.
NOT FOR NOTHING, DOC, BUT I FEEL PRETTY GOOD, CONSIDERING. HOW SOON UNTIL YOU CAN CUT ME LOOSE?
THAT WILL BE THE DILAUDID TALKING. YOU WERE VERY LUCKY, BUT YOUR WOUNDS ARE SEVERE AND WILL NEED TIME TO HEAL.
I GUESS MICHAEL CAN PICK UP THE SLACK FOR ME FOR A DAY OR TWO, BUT THERE'S NO WAY I'M LETTING HIM SIDELINE ME ON THIS RED BALL.
...JONAH... MICHAEL IS... I MEAN, HE DIDN'T...
WHAT ARE--
GET OUT. VISITING HOURS ARE OVER.
It's my fault. I should've BEEN there to back Michael up, the way I always do. Or DID. The way he TAUGHT me.
It's my fault, and I have to make it RIGHT. For the BOTH of us.

IT'S UNCANNY. HE'S JUST LIKE YOU WERE AT THAT AGE, GABRIEL.

NO, TOBIAS. HE IS A BETTER MAN THAN I'LL EVER BE. IN SPITE OF HIS... LIMITATIONS.

LIMITATIONS? JONAH'S MIRACULOUS RECOVERY WOULD SUGGEST HE'S MORE LIKE YOU THAN YOU'D CARE TO ADMIT.
HMM. MICHAEL ALWAYS SUSPECTED AS MUCH. IT'S WHY HE CHOSE TO PARTNER UP WITH JONAH...TO OBSERVE HIM, AND TAKE STOCK OF HIS POTENTIAL. BUT NOW...
MICHAEL'S DEATH LEAVES THE COUNCIL WITHOUT A LEADER. I'M PRAYING TONIGHT'S EMERGENCY MEETING WILL HELP MAINTAIN STABILITY, ONLY...
...I FEAR THE WORST IS AHEAD. WE'RE GOING TO NEED YOU IN THESE DARK TIMES, OLD FRIEND.
I'VE BEEN AWAY FROM ALL THAT FOR SO LONG, BUT I...I'LL GO, OF COURSE.

MICHAEL MUST HAVE HAD HIS SUSPICIONS ABOUT THE MOTIVES BEHIND THE MURDERS HE WAS INVESTIGATING. ALL OF THE VICTIMS WERE CONNECTED TO THE COUNCIL.
AND NOW, WITH HIS DEATH, ONE THING BECOMES PAINFULLY OBVIOUS...
YES. THE SWORD OF MALAKHIM IS IN PLAY ONCE AGAIN. SOMEONE INTENDS TO DESTROY US, AND UNDO A THOUSAND YEARS OF PEACE.

IF JONAH IS INDEED ONE OF US, THEN HE IS IN GRAVE DANGER.
ONCE WHOEVER IS BEHIND THIS PLOT LEARNS THAT JONAH IS SPECIAL, MY SON WILL BECOME A TARGET.
YOU CAN'T PROTECT HIM FOREVER, GABRIEL.
BUT SIR, JUST NOW, THE DOCTOR HIMSELF SAID HOW LUCKY I WAS THAT MY WOUNDS ARE SUPERFICIAL AND WILL HEAL IN NO TIME--!
OF COURSE YOU'RE OFF THE GLENDON CASE. I'M PUTTING YOU ON AN EXTENDED MEDICAL LEAVE! GET SOME REST. AFTER A MONTH OR TWO, WE'LL SEE WHERE WE'RE AT.
But I CAN'T rest. I won't be able to HEAL until I get to the BOTTOM of these murders. Then, maybe Michael can rest as well.
MORGUE
EXIT
4-21 ROOM PATIENT
HALL
JONAH? DAMN. I'D HEARD YOU WERE UPSTAIRS. WHAT'RE YOU DOING OUT OF BED?

HAVE THE VICTIMS FROM LAST NIGHT'S MULTIPLE BEEN PROCESSED YET? I'M LOOKING FOR A WILFRED GLENDON.
S-SURE, BUT-- YOU'RE NOT STILL WORKING THE CASE, ARE YOU?
C'MON RICHIE, WE'VE KNOWN EACH OTHER A LONG TIME. I'LL BE TWO MINUTES, TOPS. COME IN WITH ME IF YOU WANT.
WHEN I THINK OF WHAT YOU MUST BE GOING THROUGH. WITH YOUR PARTNER AND ALL, I MEAN.
HE'S HERE, YOU KNOW. MICHAEL. IF YOU WANT TO...
CAN WE PLEASE JUST... STICK TO THE MATTER AT HAND?
I KNOW THAT HAIR AND NAILS CAN CONTINUE TO GROW AFTER YOU DIE, BUT THIS--THIS IS--YOU EVER SEE SOMETHING LIKE THIS BEFORE?
M-MAYBE NOT TO THIS DEGREE, BUT YOU'D BE SURPRISED AT HOW SOME OF THE BODIES IN HERE CAN SWELL AND CHANGE, EVEN WITH REFRIGERATION.
Richie doesn't know what he's TALKING about. I've SEEN my share of DB's and this one isn't RIGHT.

WHAT ABOUT THIS HERE? THESE MARKS. PUNCTURE WOUNDS?
MMM. PROBABLY. THAT'S CONSISTENT WITH PRELIMINARY TOXICOLOGY. LIKE HE MAY HAVE BEEN DRUGGED FIRST, OR SOMETHING.
OKAY. I'M-- I'M READY TO SEE THE, UH, THE OTHER BODY NOW.
CHEST WOUND, OBVIOUSLY. THIS WAS DEFINITELY DONE WITH A SWORD. WE'VE HAD MORE THAN A FEW OF THESE IN HERE, BELIEVE IT OR NOT.
...
OH, YEAH... HE HAD THESE, BACK HERE. EXIT WOUNDS? VERY STRANGE. THIS, I HAVE NOT SEEN BEFORE.
The REALLY strange thing is -- I HAVE.

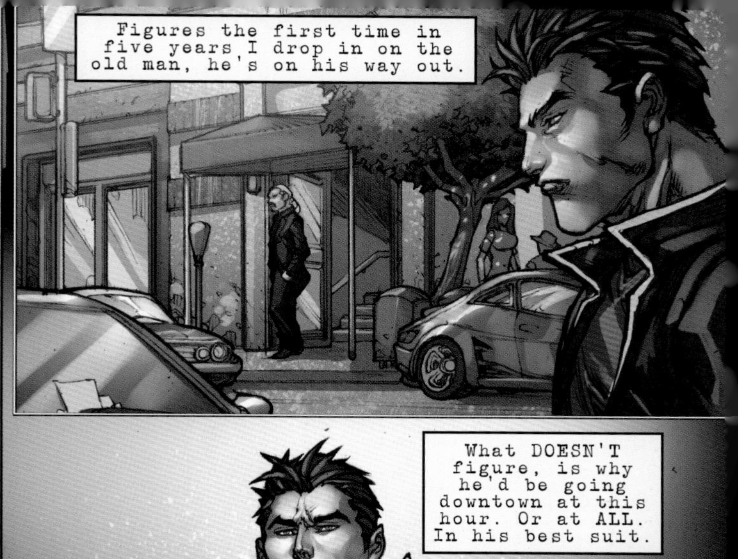
Figures the first time in five years I drop in on the old man, he's on his way out.

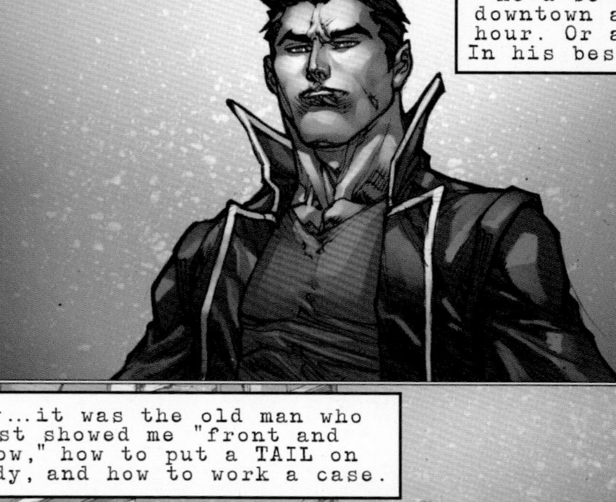
What DOESN'T figure, is why he'd be going downtown at this hour. Or at ALL. In his best suit.

Funny...it was the old man who first showed me "front and follow," how to put a TAIL on somebody, and how to work a case.
I'm looking at murders each more DEPRAVED than the last. No obvious COMMONALITY among the victims. The M.O. suggests more than one perpetrator.

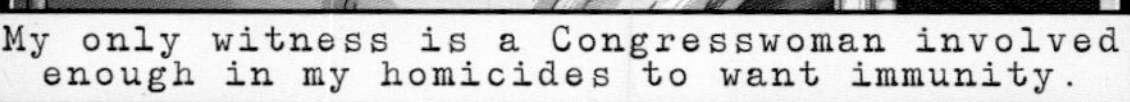
My only witness is a Congresswoman involved enough in my homicides to want immunity.

My only SUSPECT is found right where the Congresswoman SAID he'd be. Except HE'S the latest victim of the murders I LIKED him for.

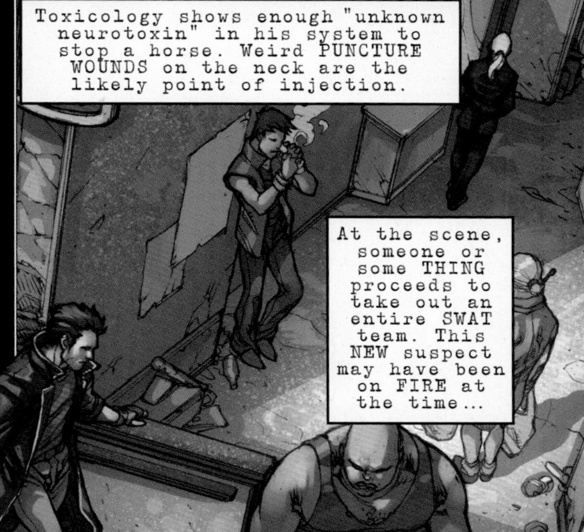
Toxicology shows enough "unknown neurotoxin" in his system to stop a horse. Weird PUNCTURE WOUNDS on the neck are the likely point of injection.
At the scene, someone or some THING proceeds to take out an entire SWAT team. This NEW suspect may have been on FIRE at the time...

WHERE ARE YOU *TAKING* ME, POP?
PRIVATE PARTY.
THIS SAYS *DIFFERENT*.
BEAT IT, PIG. WE DON'T *RECOGNIZE* YOUR AUTHORITY.
OOF!
Even if I DIDN'T just get out of the hospital, there's no way I could take on BOTH of these guys. So, it's the KITCHEN, then.
It takes serious balls to stand tough against a badge. That, or a lot of JUICE.
Either WAY, I really don't know what I'm walking INTO, here.

This place is a MAZE. It's making me dizzy. Feels like I've been walking around for hours.
Wait...didn't I just PASS this crazy painting a minute ago?
And now I'VE gone crazy, too.
YOU SHOULD HAVE STAYED AWAY. NOW WE'LL HAVE TO KILL YOU.
M-MOTHERF--!
DO YOU --RRRAGH!-- RECOGNIZE THIS AUTHORITY?!
HUNNF!

GASP!

THAT'S ENOUGH--!

GET UP.
DAD? WHAT ARE THOSE GUYS? WHAT'S GOING ON HERE? HOW'RE YOU MIXED UP IN THIS?

YEAH, WELL, DON'T GIVE ME A HAND OR ANYTHING.
LISTEN AND LISTEN GOOD, JONAH. I KNOW I WAS A SHITTY FATHER.
BUT I NEED YOU TO UNDERSTAND, EVERYTHING I DID OR DIDN'T DO -- IT WAS ALWAYS FOR YOUR OWN GOOD.

YOU COULDN'T SEE THAT THEN...AND THERE ARE THINGS HAPPENING NOW, THAT YOU WERE NEVER MEANT TO SEE.
I SAW THE CUTS ON MICHAEL'S BACK, DAD. THEY'RE THE SAME AS YOURS. WHAT'S THE CONNECTION? WHAT ARE YOU NOT TELLING ME?

I HAVE TO KNOW, DAD. IF MICHAEL'S MURDERER IS BEHIND THIS DOOR, I NEED TO KNOW THE TRUTH.

AH, GABRIEL-- AND JONAH! WELCOME! THE MEETING IS JUST ABOUT TO GET UNDERWAY.
And just like that, I'm that nervous kid all over again.
With a closet FULL of every monster imaginable...
And somewhere among them, is the one who killed my partner.

EPOCH

Chapter Two

Written by:
Kevin McCarthy

Art by:
Paolo Pantalena

Colors by:
Bill Farmer

Letters by:
Troy Peteri

THE CLOISTERS MUSEUM, NEAR THE NORTHERN TIP OF MANHATTAN.
This place was a medieval French monastery before it became a museum.
Now, someone's turned it into a MORGUE.
As a detective, scenes like this come with the territory. You get USED to it.
This time, it's different. I want to lie down and JOIN these two. Just give up. Fuck it. I Quit.
But these old buildings, they were disassembled brick-by-brick before being shipped over here and put back together. Repurposed.
TEMPUS TEMPORIS
I'm starting to feel like the same thing is happening to me...

GABRIEL. THOUGH I'M NOT SURPRISED TO SEE YOU. TOBIAS NEVER COULD MAKE A MOVE WITHOUT YOU OR MICHAEL.
I was expecting, maybe, a mobbed-up poker game, or – or some kind of kinky SEX thing, but THIS, this is...
...this is through the looking-glass and down the rabbit hole. And I'm the one in the blue dress.
DELPHIN - Leader of the Troll Order.
LILITH - Leader of the Demon Order.
MYA - Leader of the Gorgon Order.
BAD ENOUGH WE HAVE TO LIVE AMONG THEM, PRETENDING TO BE AS WEAK AS THEY ARE. I FIND THEIR PRESENCE HERE OFFENSIVE, AS SHOULD ALL OF YOU!
MS. TOKAGE?! WHAT ARE YOU--? THIS IS CRAZY...

GISELLE - Leader of the Banshee Order.
FIRST, MY PACK LEADER IS BRUTALLY MURDERED. AND THOUGH IT MADE MY BLOOD BOIL, I DIDN'T SEEK REVENGE OUT OF RESPECT FOR MICHAEL.
BUT NOW HE'S DEAD AS WELL. AND HUMANS ARE PRESENT AT OUR COUNCIL MEETING? MY PATIENCE IS AT AN END.
CYRUS - Leader of the Vampire Order.
PATIENCE OR HUMILITY, RASPUTIN? GLENDON'S DEATH MAKES YOU TOP DOG, RIGHT? WE'RE BARKING UP THE WRONG TREE HERE, WORRYING ABOUT HUMANS.
BIANCA - Leader of the Warlock Order.
TOBIAS - Leader of the Angel Order.
RASPUTIN - Acting Leader of the Werewolf Order.
WHY QUIBBLE OVER HUMANS WHEN THE MURDERS OF A WEREWOLF AND AN ARCHANGEL PRESENT A DISTURBING PATTERN?
I CONCUR. IT'S POSSIBLE THESE KILLINGS ARE MEANT TO DESTABILIZE THE PEACE OUR COUNCIL HAS KEPT FOR OVER A THOUSAND YEARS.
EXACTLY WHY I CALLED GABRIEL. DIRE CIRCUMSTANCES CALL FOR UNORTHODOX MEASURES.
WHAT'S CALLED FOR IS NEW LEADERSHIP. WE'RE AT THE END OF AN ERA -- LA FIN D'UNE EPOQUE.
IT IS TIME TO REENACT EPOCH.

NO, WE NEED TO FIND MICHAEL'S **KILLER**. GIVE US THE OPPORTUNITY TO INVESTIGATE BEFORE YOU BEGIN **EPOCH**.
AND GET TO THE BOTTOM OF THESE KILLINGS **MYSELF**.
YOU WEREWOLVES ARE BIASED AS **HELL** AGAINST MY PEOPLE, SO I JUST **KNOW** IT'LL BE A VAMPIRE AT THE SHORT END OF YOUR "INVESTIGATION."
THINK WE'RE STUPID? YOU PROBABLY KILLED GLENDON **YOURSELF**, SO YOU COULD ASSUME HIS SEAT ON THE COUNCIL.
THAT'S **ENOUGH** OUT OF YOU...
GRRAAAGGH!
GLOMMN!
HNNGH!
IS **THAT** ALL YOU'VE GOT?
HAARGHFF!

STOP THEM. THIS WILL RUIN EVERYTHING WE'VE WORKED FOR.
UNDERSTOOD.
MUCH AS I'D LOVE TO SEE THIS PLAY OUT...
STAY OUT OF THIS, DEMON. IT DOESN'T CONCERN YOU!
THIS CONCERNS ALL OF US. YOUR RAGE HAS BLINDED YOU TO THAT FACT, MAKING IT MUCH EASIER FOR ME TO DO THIS.
GRRRRARRRGH!
Still can't believe my own eyes. How can any of this be REAL?
THIS IS RIDICULOUS. WE OBVIOUSLY NEED TO FIND A NEW COUNCIL HEAD. AND SOON.
ONLY THROUGH OUR SACRED TOURNAMENT MAY WE DETERMINE WHO WILL LEAD US OUT OF THESE DARK HOURS.
WE HAVE NO CHOICE. WE MUST ENACT EPOCH NOW.

NO, NO... THE CALL FOR EPOCH IS PREMATURE. BESIDES, THE ORDER OF ANGELS HAS NO CHAMPION WITH WHICH TO COMPETE.
THAT'S YOUR PROBLEM. YOU ANGELS HAVE HAD YOUR TURN AT THE WHEEL.
FINE. I WON'T STAND IN THE WAY ANY LONGER. BUT WE MUST SEARCH FOR MICHAEL'S KILLER.
I ASK THIS COUNCIL TO GRANT GABRIEL AND HIS SON JONAH THE JURISDICTION TO FIND WHOEVER IS RESPONSIBLE.
VERY WELL, THEN. IT SEEMS THE COUNCIL WANTS CLOSURE.
THEY ARE HEREBY EMPOWERED TO INVESTIGATE THE MURDERS OF OUR COUNCIL MEMBERS. FOR THE REST OF US, EPOCH BEGINS!
IF THERE WERE ANYONE ELSE, I'D SPARE YOU THIS BURDEN. BUT IT IS OUR DARKEST HOUR. YOU KNOW WHAT'S AT STAKE HERE.
IT'S ALRIGHT. MICHAEL WOULD STILL BE HERE IF IT WEREN'T FOR MY ACTIONS. I WANT TO DO THIS... FOR HIM.
NOW PLEASE, LET'S ALL LEAVE PEACEFULLY TO PREPARE OURSELVES FOR EPOCH. AND PRAY ITS OUTCOME RINGS HOPEFUL IN ETERNITY.
LET'S GO SOMEWHERE WE CAN TALK.

WEREWOLVES? VAMPIRES? ANGELS?! AND YOU KNEW ABOUT IT THIS WHOLE TIME? NO MORE SECRETS, DAD. WHAT THE FUCK IS GOING ON HERE?
FULL DISCLOSURE. IT HASN'T BEEN EASY, KEEPING THINGS FROM YOU. WHAT YOU SAW TONIGHT IS ONLY THE LATEST CHAPTER OF A SAGA THAT SPANS THE MILLENNIA.
LET ME TELL YOU THE UNBELIEVABLE STORY OF YOUR LEGACY.
"SUPERNATURALS HAVE SHARED THE WORLD WITH MANKIND FROM THE VERY BEGINNING. AND IT WASN'T EXACTLY A SECRET THEN...
"IT'S ALL THERE IN THE RELIGIONS AND MYTHOLOGIES OF EVERY CULTURE. SUPERNATURALS HAVE INSPIRED BOTH FEAR AND WONDER IN THE HEARTS OF MAN SINCE THE DAWN OF TIME.
"BUT MOSTLY FEAR. THOUGH THE SUPERNATURALS HAD SUPERIOR ABILITIES, THE HUMANS WERE GREATER IN NUMBER.
"UNITED IN FEAR, MANKIND DROVE US TO THE BRINK OF EXTINCTION, FORCING THOSE REMAINING INTO HIDING.
"ULTIMATELY, WE UNDERSTOOD WE HAD TO GO UNDERGROUND AND BAND TOGETHER IF WE WERE TO SURVIVE."

"IT WASN'T UNANIMOUS, BUT EIGHT OF THE SUPERNATURAL RACES CAME TOGETHER AND FORMED A COUNCIL. THE LATEST VERSION OF WHICH YOU SAW FOR YOURSELF, UPSTAIRS.
"THERE'S VAMPIRES AND WEREWOLVES. WARLOCKS, BANSHEES, THE GORGONS, TROLLS, DEMONS, AND...
ANGELS? DAD, YOU CAN'T EXPECT ME TO BELIEVE THAT I'M... THAT WE'RE...AND MICHAEL IS - WAS - AN ANGEL, TOO?
HE WAS THE GREATEST OF US ALL. AN ARCHANGEL. MEANING HE WAS OF A SUPERIOR CAPABILITY AND RANK WITHIN THE ORDER OF ANGELS.
YOU SEE, NOT ALL ANGELS ARE CREATED EQUAL. AND ONLY ARCHANGELS ARE FIT TO SERVE THE ORDER AS WARRIORS.
"SO YOU'VE GOT THESE WARRING FACTIONS TENTATIVELY AGREEING TO WORK TOGETHER, BUT THAT STILL LEFT THE DELICATE TASK OF CHOOSING A LEADER.
"IT WAS DECIDED THAT THE MATTER WOULD BE SETTLED HONORABLY, IN SINGLE COMBAT.
"A CONTEST OF STRENGTH AND HEART, WHICH CAME TO BE CALLED "EPOCH." THE DAWN OF A NEW ERA.
"FROM THE GREATEST WARRIORS OF EIGHT SUPERNATURAL ORDERS WOULD RISE A CHAMPION."

"THE LAST EPOCHAL TOURNAMENT SPANNED THE GLOBE AND LITERALLY SHOOK THE EARTH WITH ITS FURY!
"AT THE END STOOD MICHAEL. IN KEEPING WITH EPOCH LAW, THE WINNER CHOOSES THE NEXT COUNCIL HEAD. THANKFULLY, MICHAEL APPOINTED HIMSELF."
NOW THAT MICHAEL'S GONE, HIS PEACEFUL TENURE IS OVER. SO THE WHOLE DAMNED THING STARTS ALL OVER AGAIN. AND THE WORLD HANGS IN THE BALANCE.
BUT HOW CAN HE HAVE DIED? IF I COULD SOMEHOW SURVIVE A HOLE PUNCHED THROUGH MY CHEST, WHY DIDN'T HE?
IT'S NOT AN EASY THING TO DO, BUT AN ANGEL CAN BE KILLED IF ONE HAS THE WILL. AND THE RIGHT WEAPON. WE CALL IT THE SWORD OF MALAKHIM.
AND, GOD FORGIVE ME, IT'S MY FAULT. I BROUGHT THE SWORD OUT OF HIDING. CUT OFF AN ANGEL'S WINGS WITH IT, AND THAT ANGEL BECOMES AS MORTAL AS...
WELL, AS MORTAL AS YOUR MOTHER WAS...AND AS I AM NOW.
THOSE SCARS ON YOUR BACK? MICHAEL HAD THEM, TOO.
I WEAR THE SCARS BY CHOICE. MICHAEL TOLD ME THE SWORD WAS TOO DANGEROUS TO BE EXPOSED, BUT I DIDN'T LISTEN. I WAS SELFISH, AND HE'S DEAD BECAUSE OF IT.

"ONCE, I WAS AN ARCHANGEL LIKE MICHAEL. AS THE FUTURE OF THE ORDER OF ANGELS, I WAS GROOMED TO SUCCEED HIM. ALL THAT CHANGED WHEN I MET YOUR MOTHER.
"THOUGH IT WAS FORBIDDEN, WE MARRIED AND STARTED A LIFE TOGETHER. BUT I KNEW TO MAKE IT WORK I COULDN'T JUST LEAVE THE ORDER. I HAD TO CAST OFF MY IMMORTALITY.
"I FIRST LEARNED ABOUT THE SWORD OF MALAKHIM FROM MY STUDIES WITH THE ORDER. ITS LOCATION WAS LOST TO THE AGES, ITS EXISTENCE THOUGHT TO BE A MYTH.
"BUT I JUST HAD TO FIND IT, AND FINALLY, IMPOSSIBLY... I DID.
"WHAT I DID NEXT WAS BOTH THE HARDEST THING I HAVE EVER DONE, AND THE EASIEST.
"AFTERWARD, I ENTRUSTED THE SWORD OF MALAKHIM TO MICHAEL, FOR SAFEKEEPING.
"HE WASN'T HAPPY ABOUT MY LEAVING THE ORDER, BUT I THINK HE UNDERSTOOD HOW MUCH YOUR MOTHER MEANT TO ME. SHE REALLY WAS AN EXTRAORDINARY WOMAN. I'D DO IT ALL AGAIN."
THE REST YOU KNOW. YOUR MOTHER DIED GIVING BIRTH TO YOU. THE BEST PARTS OF ME DIED WITH HER. AND NOW MICHAEL...WE HAVE TO BRING HIS KILLER TO JUSTICE.
I...DON'T WORRY. WE WILL. I PROMISE YOU.

THE PARK IMPERIAL, 230 WEST 56TH STREET: THE PENTHOUSE OF DR. TOBIAS ATROX AND HIS WIFE ALIYAH...
NO, TOBIAS! HOW CAN YOU EVEN CONSIDER SUCH A THING?
ALIYAH, YOU KNOW AS WELL AS I THAT IF THE ORDER OF ANGELS IS TO COMPETE IN EPOCH, WE MUST HAVE AN ARCHANGEL FOR OUR CHAMPION.
WITH MICHAEL GONE, AND GABRIEL RUINED, THAT ONLY LEAVES GABRIEL'S SON.
I CAN'T BELIEVE WHAT I'M HEARING. HE IS A HUMAN!
HALF HUMAN, WITH AN ARCHANGEL'S DNA. JONAH HAS THE POTENTIAL TO EVOLVE INTO AN ARCHANGEL. AND WITH YOUR TRAINING, COULD REPRESENT THE ORDER IN THE TOURNAMENT.
HA! NOW I KNOW YOU'RE JOKING! AND THEN WHAT? DO YOU REALLY THINK A HUMAN HAS ANY HOPE OF WINNING?
MAYBE IT'S JUST AS WELL. LET ONE OF THE OTHER CLANS LEAD THE COUNCIL FOR A CHANGE.
YOU CAN'T MEAN THAT, ALIYAH. IF ANOTHER SUPERNATURAL GROUP ASSUMES CONTROL OF THE COUNCIL, THERE'S NO GUARANTEE THEY WOULD MAINTAIN A PEACEFUL COEXISTENCE WITH HUMANS.
IF I MAY INTERJECT? PERHAPS ONE OF US COULD SERVE AS CHAMPION OF THE ORDER.

MARUT, IF YOU THINK YOU'VE GOT WHAT IT TAKES, THEN I'M SURE WE'D ALL LOVE TO SEE WHAT YOU CAN DO. RIGHT HERE, RIGHT NOW. LET'S GO.
IF YOU INSIST.
HISSST!
OOF!
CRASH
IF YOU'RE QUITE FINISHED, ALIYAH. JUST GIVE JONAH A CHANCE. THAT'S ALL I ASK. WHO KNOWS IF HE WILL EVEN AGREE TO DO IT?
BUT LET'S AT LEAST TRY. IT'S A SHAME OUR CHAMPION HAS TO BE AN ARCHANGEL, WHEN WE HAVE SO CAPABLE A FIGHTER IN YOU.
HMPH. I SUPPOSE THE HUMAN COULDN'T DO ANY WORSE THAN HE DID.

AN EXCLUSIVE LOUNGE AT 18 LITTLE WEST 12TH STREET.
After my father the archangel makes a call, we splurge for a cab to the Meatpacking District.
This place is full of vampires in both the figurative and the literal sense.
Anyone who can take on a rabid werewolf without breaking a sweat isn't someone I want to mess with, but the bite marks on Wilfred Glendon's neck obviously make him a person of interest.

GENTLEMEN...
THANKS FOR AGREEING TO SEE US ON SUCH SHORT NOTICE.
NOT A PROBLEM, REALLY. WHATEVER I CAN DO TO HELP WITH YOUR INVESTIGATION. WE ALL HAVE A VESTED INTEREST IN FINDING THE KILLER, OR KILLERS.
HOW'S THE SHOULDER DOING?

HMM? OH, THIS. AS LONG AS I DON'T START HOWLING AT THE NEXT FULL MOON, I SHOULD BE FINE.

SPEAKING OF, WILFRED GLENDON'S BODY WAS FOUND WITH SOME TELLTALE BITE MARKS ON ITS NECK.
SUGGESTING THAT YOU OR ONE OF YOUR GUYS COULD'VE HAD SOMETHING TO DO WITH HIS MURDER. WHERE WERE YOU THAT NIGHT, SAY AROUND MIDNIGHT OR SO?
BITE MARKS ...? OH, RIGHT. BECAUSE I'M A VAMPIRE. TSK-TSK! THAT'S RACIAL

RELAX. I'M ONLY PLAYING WITH YOU. I WAS HERE ALL NIGHT LAST NIGHT. MY LADIES WILL VOUCH FOR ME. FOR WHATEVER THAT'S WORTH TO YOU.
AS FOR "MY GUYS," WELL...HAVE YOU CONSIDERED THE POSSIBILITY THESE BITE MARKS WERE PUT THERE TO CAST SUSPICION IN OUR DIRECTION?
SURE. I'VE EVEN CONSIDERED THAT SUCH AN OBVIOUS CLUE COULD BE CONCLUSIVE EVIDENCE HIDDEN IN PLAIN SIGHT LIKE THE PURLOINED LETTER. BY YOU, OR SOME OTHER VAMPIRE.
BESIDES, I'M NATURALLY SUSPICIOUS OF EVERYONE.
BUT YOU'RE DEALING WITH SUPERNATURALS, NOW. THIS IS A VERY DIFFERENT WORLD THAN THE ONE YOU'RE USED TO.
I DISAGREE. I DON'T CARE IF HE CAN TURN INTO A WOLF OR A BAT; A LIAR IS STILL A LIAR. IT'S JUST A MATTER OF FOLLOWING THE FACTS TO DISCOVER IF THAT LIAR IS ALSO A KILLER.
WE'RE ALL KILLERS, DETECTIVE WRIGHT. WE HAVE TO BE. IN ORDER TO SURVIVE, A LITTLE BLOOD MUST BE SPILLED.
HOW MUCH BLOOD DID WILFRED GLENDON SPILL? A VAMPIRE WOULDN'T NEED MUCH MORE THAN THREE PINTS, GIVE OR TAKE.
STOP IT. LET-ME-GO!
YOU AREN'T GOING ANYWHERE, YOU STUPID BINT.
IT'S MY CLUB, DETECTIVE. PLEASE LET ME HANDLE THIS MY WAY.

GRIFFIN, I ONLY LET YOU IN HERE BECAUSE YOU'RE BIANCA'S BITCH.
BUT NOW, I'M GOING TO MAKE YOU *MINE*.
YOU'VE *LOST* A STEP IN YOUR VERY OLD AGE.
HUFF!
KLAPP
HARRGH!

WHAT'S *THIS* ONE? A LEPRECHAUN?

WARLOCK. THEY HAVE *ELEMENTAL* POWERS. YOUR GUN WON'T BE OF MUCH HELP AGAINST HIS DEFENSIVE "MAGIC."

Maybe not, but it'll make **ME** feel better.

THIS IS WHAT HAPPENS WHEN YOU DRINK *BLOOD* INSTEAD OF BODDINGTONS!

AAGH!

OKAY, HARRY POTTER... YOU'VE HAD YOUR FUN. HANDS WHERE I CAN *SEE* THEM.

YOU SHOULD LEARN TO MIND YOUR OWN *BUSINESS,* MATE.

WE SHOULD GET GOING.
WHAT? WE CAN'T JUST LEAVE THIS GUY HERE.
AH, DON'T WORRY ABOUT HIM. HIS PEOPLE WILL FLY OVER ON THEIR BROOMS AND SWEEP HIM UP. IT'LL BE KEPT IN-HOUSE -- NO COPS. NO OFFENSE.
NONE TAKEN.
FOLLOW THE BLOOD, DETECTIVE! BLOOD NEVER LIES.
NOW AS FOR YOU, MY DEAR...WOULD YOU CARE TO JOIN ME IN THE...VIP SECTION?
It's pretty late, but we head back uptown to Roosevelt for another look at Wilfred Glendon before calling it a night.
The whole "vampires only take three pints" thing wouldn't necessarily exclude one from my list of suspects, but it won't hurt to reexamine the body.
With my partner gone, I guess it's not so bad having the old man as back-up.
MORGUE
<EXIT
HALL -
Michael was like a BROTHER to him, and a FATHER to me. So we BOTH want the scumbag that took him from us.

SIGH JUST DON'T TAKE TOO LONG IN THERE, OKAY?
YOU'RE THE BEST, RICHIE. I'M NOT JUST SAYING THAT.
AND YOU SAID THE TOXICOLOGY SHOWED SOME KIND OF POISON?
SORT OF. AN "UNIDENTIFIED NEUROTOXIN."
ENOUGH TO TAKE THE FIGHT OUT OF ANYTHING. EVEN A WEREWOLF, I GUESS.
THAT COULD BE SOMETHING. LET'S TAKE A BLOOD SAMPLE WITH US. I THINK DELPHIN MIGHT BE ABLE TO TELL US MORE.
THAT'S THE UH... THE TROLL, RIGHT?
EVERYTHING IS A BIG JOKE TO YOU, HUH?
WAIT, WHAT? NO! ALL I ASKED WAS--!
WELL, THIS IS NOT A JOKE, JONAH. AND YOU'RE IN THIS NOW, WHETHER YOU LIKE IT OR NOT. WHETHER I LIKE IT OR NOT...

DAD...C'MON, WAIT. HAVE YOU CONSIDERED MAYBE I'M NOT MAKING A JOKE? THAT MAYBE LEARNING EVERY NIGHTMARE IN THE WORLD IS REAL MIGHT LEAVE ME WITH A FEW QUESTIONS?
BUT SINCE YOU'VE ALWAYS BEEN SO GREAT AT COMMUNICATING WITH YOUR OWN SON, WHY EVEN BOTHER, RIGHT?
LOOK, IT'S LATE. WE'VE DONE ENOUGH FOR ONE NIGHT. LET'S JUST PICK THIS UP IN THE MORNING.
WHATEVER YOU SAY, POP.
Glendon, W.
THAT'S THE FATHER. I COULD KILL HIM FROM HERE...
NO. WE NEED HIM IN PLAY FOR A LITTLE LONGER.
AND THE SON. HOW CAN THIS HUMAN POSSIBLY POSE A THREAT TO US?
THAT REMAINS T
BE SEEN.

AND THEN I GET TO KILL HIM, RIGHT?
OH, ABSOLUTELY. THAT IS, IF YOU CAN.
BUT IF NOT, IF THE RUMORS ARE TRUE ABOUT THIS JONAH WRIGHT...THEN I WILL HAVE TO KILL HIM MYSELF.

Chapter Three

Written by:
Kevin McCarthy

Art by:
Paolo Pantalena

Colors by:
Bill Farmer

Letters by:
Troy Peteri

THE CLOISTERS
NEAR THE NORTHERN TIP OF MANHATTAN.
First thing they teach you in detective school is that everyone's HIDING something.
Remembering that has served me well in my career, but hasn't made my LIFE any simpler.
Take THIS poor woman--Congresswoman Mya Tokage--much more of a mystery to me ALIVE, than dead.
Over the course of her life she kept secrets from everyone, including HERSELF. In death, she tells me almost everything I need to know.
Up here in the middle of nowhere, in the middle of the night? She was up to no good.
She wasn't expecting TROUBLE. Probably KNEW her attacker. She didn't put up a struggle. She wasn't--?! Oh, my GOD--!
TEMPUS TEMPORIS

WEEKS EARLIER, THE APARTMENT OF DETECTIVE JONAH WRIGHT.
Being asleep or awake is the same THING to me lately. Either way, there are NIGHTMARES.
I've gone over my case files. Knowing NOW that these victims were supernatural hasn't brought me closer to solving their murders.
What I DO know is, I almost became a victim myself. Instead, I lost my partner and any sense I had of who I am. Of WHAT I am...
Unless I make SENSE of this, whoever's behind these killings will cut a path towards their endgame unchallenged. With a stolen sword that can kill ANGELS.
And once Epoch begins, the body count will only grow. Maybe that's been the goal all along...but who stands to benefit most?
Memories
I dug up this old photo album for some background. It's one of the only things I took when I moved out.
No pictures of ME, but it's a glimpse into how life used to be for my parents. And Michael.
Mom looks so young. And HAPPY.
She died a few weeks after this picture was taken. The day I was born. Yeah. "Memories."
I'd like to FORGET the last week ever HAPPENED...
BZZZZT

JONAH! I HOPE WE'RE NOT DISTURBING YOU, BUT IT'S IMPORTANT WE TALK. THIS IS ALIYAH. MY WIFE.
HELLO.
WHAT, DID MY FATHER ASK YOU TO CHECK UP ON ME?

GABRIEL? NO, NO. YOU'VE BEEN THROUGH A LOT. AND NOT JUST PHYSICALLY. I'M SURE LAST NIGHT'S COUNCIL MEETING WAS A LOT TO ABSORB.

I'D LIKE TO GIVE YOU A SHOT TO AID IN YOUR RECOVERY. AND, IF YOU'RE INTERESTED, YOUR TRAINING.

NOW, YOU MAY EXPERIENCE SOME DIZZINESS OR EVEN STIFFNESS AFTERWARDS. THIS IS A POTENT COCKTAIL OF B VITAMINS.
WAIT. TRAINING? WHAT TRAINING? TRAINING FOR WHAT?

TO REPRESENT THE ORDER OF ANGELS IN EPOCH. AS OUR FIGHTER. WE HAVE TO HAVE AN ARCHANGEL, AND YOU'RE THE LAST LIVING CARRIER OF THAT GENETIC STRAIN.
IT'S SOMETHING MICHAEL WOULD'VE WANTED. WE'D DISCUSSED YOU BECOMING HIS SUCCESSOR. IF YOU'RE WILLING, ALIYAH WILL TRAIN AND PREPARE YOU FOR THE ORDEAL AHEAD.

ME? NO. NO, THAT'S -- HOW COULD I POSSIBLY--? YOU WANT ME TO FIGHT AGAINST... MONSTERS? IT'D BE SUICIDE.
I MEAN, I'D LIKE TO HELP. AND I AM. WITH THE INVESTIGATION. BUT...COMPETE WITH SUPERNATURAL CREATURES? I'M JUST A MAN.
JONAH, I KNOW YOU FEEL RESPONSIBLE FOR MICHAEL'S DEATH AND WANT TO FIND WHO DID IT. WE ALL DO.
FINDING WHOEVER'S BEHIND WON'T BRING HIM BACK. BUT BY TAKING HIS PLACE, YOU CAN AVENGE HIM! YOU CAN WIN EPOCH, APPOINT A WORTHY COUNCIL LEADER, AND PRESEVE THE PEACE MICHAEL WORKED SO HARD TO ACHIEVE.
I TOLD YOU THIS WAS A BAD IDEA. TAKES MORE THAN A FEW DROPS OF ARCHANGEL BLOOD IN THE HUMAN GENE POOL TO MAKE A WARRIOR OUT OF A WEAKLING.
SHE'S RIGHT. I BARELY SURVIVED MY FIRST SUPERNATURAL ENCOUNTER. WOULDN'T STAND A CHANCE AGAINST REAL CHAMPIONS.
MAYBE IF THERE WASN'T A GAPING HOLE IN MY CHEST. BUT EVEN THEN...
REALLY? LET'S HAVE A LOOK.
SHIRRIPPT
BUT -- BUT...HOW? I FELT...
HMM. MAYBE YOU'RE RIGHT, TOBIAS. IF HE CAN HEAL HIMSELF, MAYBE I CAN WORK WITH HIM.
AND IF I CAN HELP HIM UNLEASH HIS FULL POTENTIAL, THEN HE COULD BECOME A CHAMPION.

I SHOULD'VE WARNED YOU OF MY WIFE'S AGGRESSIVE TENDENCIES. THEY'RE WHAT MAKE HER SUCH A SUCCESSFUL TRAINER.
WE'VE GIVEN YOU A LOT TO THINK ABOUT. BUT DON'T TAKE TOO LONG. THOUGH YOU MAY BE THE LAST OF THE ARCHANGELS, YOU STILL HAVE A LOT OF WORK AHEAD OF YOU.
I head to the precinct for the latest on my case. I need to get my head back into some real-world normalcy for a minute.
Detectives Wheelock and Williams are working my cases while I'm on medical leave. And here I am, continuing to investigate against orders.
NYPD
OH! LOOK AT THIS GUY. READY TO COME BACK TO WORK? DO ME A FAVOR AND TAKE BACK YOUR STONE COLD WHODUNIT?
WRIGHT, WHY THE FUCK AREN'T YOU ON A BOAT SOMEWHERE?
GUESS I'M JUST AN ASSHOLE. GOT ANYTHING NEW ON MY MURDERS?
OH, YOU'LL LOVE THIS. WE'VE GOT AN EYEWITNESS SAYS HE SAW OUR DOER. YEAH. PREPARED TO GIVE US A FULL WRITTEN STATEMENT, TOO. IN CRAYON.
THAT'S HIM NOW? IN THE BOX? OKAY IF I TALK WITH HIM?
SHIT, BE MY GUEST. YOU CAN TYPE UP MY REPORT FOR ME TOO, IF YOU LIKE.

THE DETECTIVES SAID YOU SAW WHAT HAPPENED? WHY DON'T YOU TELL ME WHAT YOU KNOW?

I KNOW THINGS. I KNOW **SECRETS**. I'VE BEEN AROUND. I'VE SEEN THINGS. I SAW RONALD REAGAN EATING JELLYBEANS WITH AN ALIEN JESUS.

WHY DON'T WE STICK TO WHAT YOU SAW THE OTHER NIGHT?
THAT **WAS** THE OTHER NIGHT! I ALSO SAW A SNAKE LADY DRIVING A NICE CAR. AND I SAW A DEVIL MADE OF **BLUE FIRE** KILL AN ANGEL, NEAR THE WEST SIDE HIGHWAY.

WAIT A MINUTE. TELL ME **MORE** ABOUT THIS..."DEVIL."
LIKE A CAN OF **STERNO**, HE WAS! ON **FIRE**. ALL BLUE, AND LAUGHING AS THE ANGEL FELL FROM **HEAVEN**.
YOU **BELIEVE** ME, DON'T YOU? I'M NOT **CRAZY**. AREN'T YOU GOING TO WRITE ANY OF THIS DOWN?

If he's crazy... I'M crazy.
I KEEP IT ALL UP **HERE**. LIKE YOU. YOU'VE BEEN **VERY** HELPFUL, SIR. I'LL HAVE A UNIFORM DRIVE YOU TO WHEREVER YOU'D LIKE.
I'VE GOT SOME FAMILY IN **ATLANTIS**...

SORRY WE DON'T HAVE ANYTHING CONCRETE FOR YOU. WE WANT TO DO **RIGHT** BY YOU, AND **MICHAEL**. WE **ALL** FEEL HIS LOSS.
THANKS, MAN. I'M **CONFIDENT** SOMETHING'LL BREAK SOON.
DID YOU KNOW YOUR **FATHER'S** BEEN HERE ALL AFTERNOON? WASN'T SURE WHAT TO **DO** WITH HIM, SO I SAT HIM DOWN AT YOUR DESK.

THEY WOULDN'T LET ME INTERVIEW THE HOBO. HE HAVE ANYTHING INTERESTING TO SAY?
WELL, I THINK I KNOW HOW REAGAN WAS ELECTED TO TWO TERMS.
HE ALSO SAID A BURNING MAN KILLED MICHAEL, AND IT MADE ME REMEMBER A LITTLE MORE ABOUT THAT NIGHT. DOES THAT MAKE ANY SENSE TO YOU, DAD?
WHEN DEMONS USE THEIR ABILITIES, THEY SECRETE A HIGHLY-FLAMMABLE SUBSTANCE THAT CAN BE IGNITED, AND USED IN A VARIETY OF DESTRUCTIVE WAYS.
THE SPECIFIC COLOR OF THE FLAME CAN BE USED TO HELP IDENTIFY OUR MAN. NARROW THE FIELD OF SUSPECTS A BIT.
THE GUY WE LIKE FOR THIS BURNS BLUE. DO WE PICK A FIGHT WITH EVERY DEMON UNTIL WE FIND A FEW THAT FIT THE PROFILE?
MANY DEMONS BURN THAT COLOR, BUT THEY WILL ALL BE PRESENT FOR EPOCH. SEEING THEM THERE MAY HELP JOG YOUR MEMORY.
THAT REMINDS ME. OUR FRIEND THE DOCTOR PAID ME A HOUSE CALL. WANTS ME TO COMPETE IN EPOCH.
IT'S A TREMENDOUS HONOR. BUT IT'S JUST TOO DANGEROUS, SON.
EPOCH IS OUR BEST CHANCE OF GETTING ANSWERS, BUT NOT AS SPECTATORS. WOULD MICHAEL WANT ME TO WATCH AS A FLAMING MANIAC PUSHED THE COUNCIL TO CHAOS?
HE'D WANT YOU SAFE. ISN'T THAT THE POINT OF THIS ST. MICHAEL MEDALLION? PATRON SAINT OF POLICE OFFICERS. YOU WEREN'T WEARING IT THE NIGHT HE DIED, WERE YOU?
HE ALWAYS BUSTED MY CHOPS ABOUT THAT THING. SAID IT WAS A TERRIBLE LIKENESS. I THOUGHT HE WAS KIDDING. ANYWAY, TRY NOT TO LEAVE A MESS.
MICHAEL WOULDN'T WANT EPOCH FOR YOU, AND NEITHER DO I. WE'LL HONOR HIS MEMORY BY BRINGING HIS KILLER TO JUSTICE.
LISTEN! MEET ME AT THE MUSEUM OF NATUR HISTORY AT CLOSING WANT US TO FOLLO UP ON THAT NEUROTOXIN LEAD.

YOU AGAIN? STAY BACK, LADY.
HAVE YOU THOUGHT ABOUT WHAT TOBIAS AND I DISCUSSED WITH YOU? WILL YOU EMBRACE YOUR RIGHTFUL HERITAGE?
I KNOW WHAT'S AT STAKE FOR THE ORDER, AND FOR THE WORLD. AND I'M STILL NOT SURE I CAN BE THIS...WARRIOR YOU NEED ME TO BE. BUT I HAVE TO TRY, RIGHT? FOR MICHAEL.
NYPD
GOOD.
WHAT-WHAT ARE YOU DOING? LET GO OF ME--!
WHAT IF--?!
IF SOMEONE WERE TO SEE US? PLEASE. THIS IS NEW YORK CITY. NOBODY LOOKS UP ANYMORE.
BUT JUST IN CASE THEY DID, I'M MOVING MUCH TOO FAST FOR THE HUMAN EYE, OR A CAMERA, TO VIEW!

WHERE--? DID I BLACK OUT? WHAT *IS* THIS PLACE?
WE'RE DEEP INSIDE A DORMANT VOLCANO ON THE ISLAND OF CORSICA. IT'S A PROVING GROUND FOR THE ORDER OF ANGELS. A *PLACE* CAN BE SUPERNATURAL TOO, AND TIME PASSES DIFFERENTLY HERE. A MINUTE FEELS MORE LIKE A FEW HOURS.
NO TIME TO FULLY PREPARE YOU FOR *EPOCH*, BUT I CAN TEACH YOU ENOUGH SO YOU DON'T EMBARRASS YOURSELF BEFORE YOU GET KILLED.
WHY DON'T YOU START WITH THE RULES? AM I SERIOUSLY FIGHTING TO THE *DEATH* HERE, OR ARE YOU JUST MESSING WITH ME?
IT COULDN'T BE SIMPLER. TWO UNARMED COMBATANTS FIGHT EACH OTHER UNTIL ONE SUBMITS. OR IS KILLED.
CRICK
NGH! JESUS, THAT'S SOME --!
NOT BAD. BUT YOU'RE DROPPING YOUR HANDS TOO SOON. I CAN SHOW YOU HOW TO *FIX* THAT...
UM... THANKS? YOU'RE NOT SO *BAD* YOURSELF.

YES-- I *AM*!
KRAK
WHUH-- **UNGH!**
BETTER. WHERE'D YOU LEARN THAT MOVE?
MICHAEL SHOWED ME A FEW THINGS OVER THE YEARS. I DIDN'T THINK TOO MUCH OF IT AT THE TIME. COULD IT BE HE WAS TESTING ME? ***PREPARING*** ME, EVEN?
I WOULDN'T PUT IT PAST HIM.
HE ALWAYS SAW THE BIGGER PICTURE. IT'S WHAT MADE HIM A GREAT FIGHTER AND LEADER.
TWO THINGS I'LL ***NEVER*** BE. I MEAN, WHO ARE WE KIDDING?
TSK! I'VE ARRANGED A SPARRING PARTNER FOR YOU.
MARUT?

AGKH!
I DON'T SUPPOSE WE CAN TALK THIS OVER LIKE GENTLEMEN--?
WE CAN TALK ALL YOU WANT. AFTER I TEACH YOU A LESSON.
Then something weird happens. A rush of adrenaline on an almost emotional level. I taste METAL.
It's intoxicating. Like a drunk who's ready to fight the whole bar. Except there's also a clarity of mind I've never experienced before.
Is this how Michael felt? Is this what Dad gave up? It's AMAZING.
LESSON LEARNED, I'D SAY.

KIAI!
AN IMPROVEMENT. WE'VE ALREADY MADE PROGRESS! CAN YOU SENSE IT? DO YOU FEEL ANY DIFFERENT?
I THINK SO, YEAH. I'M FEELING...IT'S DIFFICULT TO PUT INTO WORDS...
OOF!
GASP!
SUCH SPEED! HE SHOULDN'T HAVE BEEN ABLE TO SURPRISE ME LIKE THAT.
JONAH'S DEVELOPING FASTER THAN EXPECTED. MAYBE HE COULD BE OUR CHAMPION...
I STILL SENSE SOME HESITANCY. THAT'LL COST YOU IN A REAL MATCH.
UM...UH... SORRY.
I THINK THAT'S ENOUGH...TRAINING FOR ONE DAY.

THE MUSEUM OF NATURAL HISTORY, JUST AFTER CLOSING.
Even after what felt like a week's worth of intense workout, I'm somehow MORE refreshed than when I started. What's Tobias doing here?
I JUST WISH YOU'D COME TO ME FIRST BEFORE APPROACHING JONAH THE WAY YOU DID.
GABRIEL, YOU KNOW WHAT CAN GO WRONG IF CONTROL OF THE COUNCIL FALLS TO ONE OF THE OTHER CLANS.
BESIDES, ALIYAH'S ALREADY BEEN WORKING WITH HIM. SHE SEES REAL POTENTIAL THERE.
I WAS, UH, JUST FILLING TOBIAS IN ON WHERE WE ARE WITH THE INVESTIGATION. DELPHIN'S AGREED TO ANALYZE THE TOXIN WE FOUND IN WILFRED GLENDON'S BODY. DID YOU BRING IT?
SIGH YES, POP.
HOW DID IT GO WITH ALIYAH TODAY? SPEAKING FROM PERSONAL EXPERIENCE, SHE CAN BE A BIT OF A TASKMASTER! BUT YOU'RE IN VERY GOOD HANDS...
GREAT, BECAUSE I FEEL LIKE I NEED INSURANCE AFTER ONE AFTERNOON WITH HER.
COME ON. DELPHIN'S WAITING...
GOOD HUNTING, GENTLEMEN!

NOW, THIS GUY DOESN'T LIKE PEOPLE AND HATES VISITORS. HE'S DOING US A BIG FAVOR BY SEEING US, SO DON'T GIVE ME ANY GRIEF, OKAY?
JESUS, WHAT'S UP YOUR ASS, ALL OF A SUDDEN? Y'KNOW, I'VE MANAGED A DECENT CAREER AS A DETECTIVE ALL THESE YEARS WITHOUT YOU HOLDING MY HAND, "DAD."
IT'S JUST--I'M JUST NOT COMFORTABLE WITH THE IDEA OF YOU FIGHTING IN THE TOURNAMENT.
CAN WE TALK ABOUT IT LATER? LET'S SEE WHAT THE TROLL LIVING UNDER THE "SUPERNATURAL HISTORY MUSEUM" HAS FOR US.
YOU'RE LATE, GABRIEL.
AND I APOLOGIZE. WE REALLY DO APPRECIATE YOU OFFERING YOUR TIME AND EXPERTISE TO OUR INVESTIGATION.
OF COURSE. WE ALL WANT TO SEE JUSTICE DONE FOR THESE VILE MURDERS. AND MICHAEL WAS A FRIEND TO THE TROLLS.
SO WE'RE JUST GIVING HIM GLENDON'S BLOOD? NO OFFENSE, BUT HOW DO WE KNOW WE CAN TRUST YOU?
JONAH...
NO, IT'S A FAIR QUESTION. THE ANSWER IS: YOU DON'T KNOW IF YOU CAN TRUST ME. UNFORTUNATELY FOR YOU, YOU ALSO DON'T KNOW SUPERNATURAL HEMATOLOGY. SO, GIVE IT HERE.
I KNOW ABOUT ARCHANGEL PHYSIOGNOMY, AS WELL. YOU'VE BEEN TRAINING, HAVEN'T YOU? FOR EPOCH? YOU'VE ALREADY TAKEN YOUR FIRST EVOLUTIONARY STEPS FORWARD.
YEAH? YOU CAN SEE ALL THAT JUST BY LOOKING AT ME, HUH?
IT TAKES TESTICULAR FORTITUDE FOR AN OUTSIDER TO WANT TO PARTICIPATE. EVEN A FLEDGLING ANGEL SUCH AS YOURSELF. TOO BAD A TROLL WILL TAKE IT THIS TIME AROUND...
BUT YOUR INVOLVEMENT MAKES THINGS THAT MUCH MORE INTERESTING. NOW, IF YOU'LL EXCUSE ME? I TRUST YOU CAN FIND YOUR WAY OUT. I SHOULD HAVE THE RESULTS IN A COUPLE OF DAYS.

TOBIAS SAID I'D FIND YOU HERE. I HOPE YOU DON'T MIND. I THOUGHT WE COULD FIT IN SOME MORE WORK, THAT IS, IF YOU'RE ALL FINISHED HERE.
UH...SURE. WE WERE JUST WRAPPING UP. RIGHT, POP?
...
OH, I DON'T LIKE THE LOOKS OF THIS. IN FACT, I THINK I'VE SEEN ENOUGH.
MAY I HAVE A QUICK WORD WITH YOU? PRIVATELY.
I'VE FELT IT TOO, YOU KNOW. THE MAGNETISM OF THE HUMAN SPIRIT. IRRESISTIBLE, ISN'T IT? NOTHING LIKE WHAT WE KNOW AS ANGELS, HMM?
MAYBE I'M IMAGINING THINGS, AND THERE'S NOTHING TO WORRY ABOUT. I ONLY ASK THAT YOU THINK VERY CAREFULLY BEFORE YOU ALLOW THINGS TO GO TOO FAR WITH MY SON.
IF YOU'RE UP FOR IT, TONIGHT, I WAS THINKING I'D PUT YOU TO THE FIRE TEST.
SOUNDS... PAINFUL.

PLEASE PLACE YOUR HAND IN THIS BASIN OF LAMP OIL. ARE YOU FAMILIAR WITH THE NAME *THICH QUANG DUC?*
SURE. HE WAS THAT VIETNAMESE BUDDHIST MONK WHO BURNED HIMSELF TO DEATH. RAGE AGAINST THE MACHINE.
HE WAS ALSO ONE OF US. AN **ANGEL** PROTESTING THE CORRUPT *DIEM* REGIME.
SO, HE DIDN'T DIE?
NO, BUT HE COULD FEEL **PAIN**; THE TRUE ENEMY OF AN IMMORTAL. ESPECIALLY IN COMBAT.
PAIN **INHIBITS**, AND CAN KEEP AN ARCHANGEL WARRIOR FROM BEING THE BEST VERSION OF HIMSELF.
CONQUERING PAIN IS SIMPLY MIND OVER MATTER. YOU MUST SEPARATE THE TWO AND CHAMPION YOURSELF! THIS IS THE FIRE TEST.
IF THE PAIN BECOMES UNBEARABLE, THERE'S ALOE WATER IN THE BASIN ON THE RIGHT. BUT THERE **IS** NO PAIN! *THICH QUANG DUC* BURNED FOR **TEN MINUTES** WITHOUT MOVING OR CRYING OUT.
ARCHANGELS HAVE THIS ABILITY TO VARYING DEGREES, BUT CAN IMPROVE WITH CONCENTRATION. STAY WITH ME JONAH. YOU CAN *DO* THIS.
HNNGH--!
GASP!
TSSSS

LATER...
GOOD.
GOOD!
BETTER!
UHH!
ARE YOU OKAY? I'M SORRY, ALIYAH.
DON'T BE. I'M IMPRESSED THAT A HUMAN -- OR, HALF-HUMAN -- GOT THE BETTER OF ME.
DID IT OCCUR TO YOU MY HUMANITY MIGHT BE A STRENGTH, NOT A WEAKNESS?
LET'S HOPE SO. THE FIRST ROUND OF EPOCH BEGINS TONIGHT.

THE AVENUE OF THE DEAD, TEOTIHUACAN, IN THE BASIN OF MEXICO.
You can FEEL the reverence for tradition. Strange to think this has gone on since before these pyramids were even built.
Stranger STILL that a cop who'd never left the five boroughs is now a part of this.
I'D HOPED WE'D HAVE MORE TIME BEFORE EPOCH BEGAN. EVEN IN THE SLOWED-DOWN ENVIRONMENT OF THE PROVING GROUNDS, I CAN'T TEACH YOU ALL YOU NEED TO KNOW.
CAN'T WE TAILOR MY TRAINING FOR THE SPECIFIC OPPONENTS I'M SCHEDULED TO FACE? LIKE CRAMMING FOR AN EXAM.
WE CAN'T KNOW FOR SURE WHO YOU'LL FACE IN THE FIRST ROUND. PROBABLY A TROLL. OR A WARLOCK. EITHER WAY, IT WON'T BE EASY.
YES, BUT, OUR TIME TOGETHER HAS-- I DON'T KNOW --AWAKENED A POTENTIAL IN ME I NEVER KNEW I HAD.
AND BEING HERE, FEELING THE PRIMAL ENERGY OF THE CROWD? I NEED TO BE A PART OF IT.
THERE'S CYRUS. NOT AN EASY GUY TO READ, BUT CHARMING AS HELL. I GUESS THAT'S A VAMPIRE FOR YOU. WHO'S THE BAD-ASS?
RAFAEL. AN AZTEC WARRIOR WHO LONG AGO KILLED MANY WOULD-BE CONQUISTADORS ON THIS VERY SPOT. EVEN WITH HIS MASTERY OF CAPOEIRA, HE HAS HIS WORK CUT OUT FOR HIM WITH DAMIEN.
YOU GOT THIS. DON'T TRY ANYTHING CUTE. JUST END THIS FUCKER AND THE DRINKS ARE ON ME.
HOW LONG HAVE WE WAITED FOR THIS NIGHT, DAMIEN? HOW LONG WILL YOU SUFFER IF YOU DON'T BRING VICTORY TO THE DEMONIC ORDER?
NOTHING CAN STAND IN THE WAY OF WHAT HAS ALREADY BEEN SET IN MOTION, QUEEN LILITH.

¡DESPERTA FERRO!
¡LES FERES TENEN FAM!
WHOOOMPH
LET'S PLAY!
IT'S BEEN TOO LONG SINCE BLOOD WAS SPILLED IN THIS SACRED PLACE. THE GODS WILL HAVE THEIR TRIBUTE TONIGHT!
PRAY TO WHOMEVER YOU LIKE. NO ONE CAN SAVE YOU NOW!
And just like that, there he is. My "devil made of BLUE FIRE."
I don't NEED to see another demon. He's the one.

GUH! I PROMISE YOU A GLORIOUS DEATH!
GRARGH!
HUH-HUH-HA-HAH!
SLISSH
FROOOSSH
YAAGGH!
SEE HOW THEY'RE BOTH USING BRAZILIAN STYLES? DAMIEN'S GRACIE JIU-JITSU HAS GOTTEN LAZY, THOUGH. HE'S RELYING TOO MUCH ON HIS FIRE. YOU CAN EXPLOIT THAT. ARE YOU EVEN LISTENING TO ME?
Such savagery. And RAGE. I'm expected to compete with THAT?
If Rafael wins, I may never get the CHANCE to question Damien...
But if DAMIEN wins, and he IS Michael's killer...God help me, but I'll FIND the rage. And welcome the chance EPOCH gives me to repay him in kind!

YOU SEE? HE'S TAPPING OUT. IT'S OVER.

SHA-RRIIPT

BUT, WHY WOULD--? SHOULDN'T DAMIEN BE DISQUALIFIED?

UNTIL A FIGHTER OFFICIALLY SUBMITS, HE'S FAIR GAME. THOSE ARE THE RULES OF ***EPOCH***. THAT'S THE NATURE OF THE BEAST.

WHAT THE FUCK ***BULLSHIT*** IS THIS, LILITH? MY MAN TRIED TO FORFEIT FAIRLY! THE FIGHT WAS ***OVER!***

NO RULES WERE BROKEN HERE. RAFAEL KNEW THE RISKS, CYRUS. AS DO YOU.

EPOCH

Chapter Four

Written by:
Kevin McCarthy

Art by:
Paolo Pantalena

Colors by:
Bill Farmer

Letters by:
Troy Peteri

THE AVENUE OF THE DEAD, TEOTIHUACAN.

Still in Mexico. Still taking part in a fighting tournament that will decide the fate of the world.

Damien is a BEAST. The more punishment he takes, the more he LOVES it. How do you stop someone like that?
HUNGGH! HA-HA-HAH!
JESUS, THIS THING COULD GO ON FOREVER.
NO, I THINK RAFAEL IS CLOSE TO TAPPING OUT. MOST LOSING FIGHTERS SUBMIT IN THE RING, AND HE'S ABOUT HAD IT.

NNARRGGH!
HISST!
HNNGG--!

YOU SEE? HE'S TAPPING OUT. IT'S OVER.

SHA-RRIPT

BUT, WHY WOULD--? SHOULDN'T DAMIEN BE DISQUALIFIED?
UNTIL A FIGHTER OFFICIALLY SUBMITS, HE'S FAIR GAME. THOSE ARE THE RULES OF EPOCH. THAT'S THE NATURE OF THE BEAST.

WHAT THE FUCK BULLSHIT IS THIS, LILITH? MY MAN TRIED TO FORFEIT FAIRLY! THE FIGHT WAS OVER!
NO RULES WERE BROKEN HERE. RAFAEL KNEW THE RISKS, CYRUS. AS DO YOU.

I KNOW DAMIEN KILLED MICHAEL TOO. BUT I CAN'T PROVE IT. HE'S A MONSTER.
NO, HE'S A DEMON. HIS BRAZILIAN JIU-JITSU AND FIRE ABILITIES ARE FORMIDABLE, BUT NOT UNBEATABLE. MICHAEL PROVED THAT. NOW IT'S YOUR TURN.

DEEP INSIDE A DORMANT VOLCANO ON THE ISLAND OF CORSICA.

HERE INSIDE THE DOME, WE'LL TEST YOUR PRIMAL INSTINCTS AND INTUITION. YOU'LL HAVE TO *FEEL* WHERE THE ATTACKS ARE COMING FROM.

ATTACKS? *PLURAL?*

FA-ROOOOSHH

DON'T HOLD *BACK*, BROTHERS. WE'LL MAKE AN *ARCHANGEL* OF HIM YET!

CRACK
KLACKT
RAAGH!
YES! BUT NOT SO *WILD*. LET YOUR OTHER SENSES GUIDE YOUR MOVEMENTS INTO A FOCUSED RESPONSE.

SWISH
THAT'S IT! AND WITH THE TANINZUDORI TECHNIQUE. PERFECT!
I THINK YOU'RE READY FOR YOUR FIRST ROUND OF *EPOCH*.

SALISBURY PLAIN, IN THE ENGLISH COUNTY OF WILTSHIRE.
Stonehenge. Through the ages, man has wondered at its true purpose.
Now I know these pillars were placed here to mark a hallowed Epoch battleground.
WHY IS THE TURNOUT SO MUCH SMALLER THAN IN MEXICO?
DON'T WORRY ABOUT THE PEOPLE. YOU HAVE A LOT TO PROVE TONIGHT.
THERE'S DAMIEN...
DON'T EVEN LOOK AT HIM! FOCUS YOUR ENERGY, OR YOU'VE ALREADY LOST.
YOUR OPPONENT IS A WARLOCK. ILLUSIONS, LEVITATION, AND ELEMENTAL ENERGY. GRIFFIN IS ALSO A MASTER OF KUNG FU.
GRIFFIN --?
THAT'S RIGHT, PALLY. YOU AND ME HAVE UNFINISHED BUSINESS.
BRUKK
THINK YOU CAN TAKE ME? LET'S SEE IF YOU'VE GOT THE STONES!
UNGH!

AARGH!
KRUKK
WHERE'S ALL YOUR SMART TALK NOW? "HARRY POTTER" MY ARSE!
MAKING ME - ME! - FIGHT A LOWLY HUMAN? WHY, IT'S AN INSULT, IS WHAT IT IS!
WELL, I'LL SHOW THEM AND THEIR SHITE COUNCIL--!
I'LL SHOW THEM ALL WHAT REAL MAGIC CAN DO!
SHRA-ZACKT
ARCHANGEL.
WHUDD
UHNNF!
LOWLY HALF-ARCHANGEL.

CHH!
KRAK
WHACK
CRACK
THUD

I have to admit, that felt fucking amazing.

YOU FOUGHT WELL. BUT IT ONLY GETS TOUGHER FROM HERE ON OUT.

COME ON. DAMIEN'S JUST TRYING TO GET IN YOUR HEAD BECAUSE YOU *SHOWED* HIM SOMETHING TODAY.

IT'S A SHAME WE BROKE STONEHENGE.
THE WARLOCK ORDER WILL RESTORE THE PILLARS TO NORMAL. THIS ISN'T THE FIRST TIME EPOCH HAS TAKEN PLACE HERE.
AND YOU'RE SURE? IF WE'RE GOING TO BRING EVIDENCE BEFORE THE COUNCIL, WE HAVE TO BE *CERTAIN.*
THE NEUROTOXIN YOU FOUND IN GLENDON'S BLOOD IS DEFINITELY GORGON VENOM. AND IT CONTAINS ENOUGH DNA TO COMPARE AGAINST A SUSPECT'S SAMPLE.
THAT MEANS IT WAS PROBABLY MYA TOKAGE, OR HER CHAMPION NYX.
WE'D ONLY NEED ONE DNA SAMPLE, THEN, TO KNOW WHICH.
JONAH FACES NYX IN THE NEXT ROUND. BUT IN ORDER TO GET A SAMPLE OF HER VENOM...
...YOU'D HAVE TO LET NYX *BITE* YOU.
AND BE PARALYZED DURING THE FIGHT? THAT'S SUICIDE.
NOT NECESSARILY. IT'S RISKY, TO BE SURE, BUT IF TIMED PROPERLY? IT *COULD* WORK.
NO! WE MUST SECURE THE NEXT EPOCH CHAMPION AND MAINTAIN OUR LEADERSHIP OF THE COUNCIL. *NOTHING* ELSE--NOT EVEN FINDING MICHAEL'S KILLER -- IS MORE IMPORTANT.
THEN WE'LL JUST HAVE TO FIND ANOTHER WAY.

THE PROVING GROUNDS.

TODAY'S TEST IS PART OF YOUR **FORCED EVOLUTION** INTO AN ARCHANGEL. WE CALL IT "FIGHT OR FLIGHT." AND IF DONE CORRECTLY, YOU'LL SPROUT YOUR **WINGS**.

YOU'VE GOT TO BE KIDDING ME. I GET TO HAVE WINGS?

SHINNG

NO. YOU HAVE TO **EARN** THEM!

KLANK

UNDER EXTREME DURESS, ARCHANGELS ARE CAPABLE OF 100X THE ADRENALINE RUSH OF A NORMAL HUMAN. THIS RESPONSE SHOULD HELP YOUR WINGS TO BURST FORTH, IF YOU HAVE IT WITHIN YOU.

AAAAAAAH!

NO WINGS.
SORRY...

WE'LL KEEP TRYING.

AN ABANDONED SUB-LEVEL OF GRAND CENTRAL TERMINAL, NYC.
KROOOM
Epoch rages on, with Damien emerging as the early favorite. A small part of me wants GRIM here, the Troll champion, to waste him and be DONE with it.
But the rest of me wants Damien all to myself.
CHUKKT
Be careful what you wish for.
OUR TIMETABLE'S BEEN PUSHED UP. YOU'RE FIGHTING NYX TONIGHT, ON HER TURF.
WHAT? WHY?
MY GUESS? SOME ON THE COUNCIL ARE EMBARRASSED YOU'VE LASTED THIS LONG IN THE TOURNAMENT, AND THEY WANT TO RUSH YOU INTO AN EARLY DEFEAT.

ANGOR WAT TEMPLE COMPLEX, CAMBODIA.
And to think I used to complain about having to drive out to Queens to follow up on a lead.
NYX'S FIGHTING STYLE IS NINJUTSU.
I've got to let her bite me. It's the only way.
THAT MEANS DIRTY TRICKS. SHE MIGHT EVEN FEIGN INJURY TO LURE YOU IN, SO YOU'LL LET DOWN YOUR GUARD.
Shouldn't be too hard, since that's what she does. But if I want to WIN, I'll have to wait until I've got her on the ropes.
DON'T BE FOOLED. AND WHATEVER YOU DO, DON'T LET HER BITE YOU! REMEMBER YOUR TRAINING.
RIGHT. ANYTHING ELSE?
DON'T GET KILLED.
HISSSSSSSAAHH!

All the training in the WORLD doesn't quite prepare you to fight a crazy monster snake lady.
KLONK
SSSSAAAHH!
FUCK--!
SNAP
AGKH!
I'm not paralyzed. Why am I not paralyzed? I should be paralyzed.
She's just as surprised as I am.

BAM
Christ, she's heavy.

WHAMM
UFF!

MY GOD, SON -- THAT WAS AMAZING.

THANKS. I FEEL SICK...
*

HARBOR VIEW TERRACE, 525 W. 55TH STREET, NYC.
I wake up in my apartment.
WE'VE GOT TO STOP MEETING LIKE THIS, POP.
AS WE SPEAK, DELPHIN IS COMPARING THE VENOM IN YOUR BLOOD AGAINST THE SAMPLE TAKEN FROM WILFRED GLENDON.
IT'S ONLY A MATTER OF TIME BEFORE WE FIGURE OUT WHO KILLED HIM, AND PROBABLY THE OTHERS, TOO.
HOW DO YOU FEEL?
LIKE I WENT TWELVE ROUNDS WITH A DINOSAUR. BUT HOW COME I FEEL ANYTHING? WHY DIDN'T THE NEUROTOXIN AFFECT ME?
OBVIOUSLY, IT DID. JUST NOT AS STRONGLY AS IT SHOULD HAVE.
MAYBE DELPHIN KNOWS WHY. I'M MEETING HIM IN A BIT TO GO OVER THE RESULTS OF THE GORGON DNA COMPARISON. GET SOME REST, OKAY?
...
MYA? WHAT ARE YOU DOING HERE? HOW --?
LET'S TAKE A RIDE.

BZZZT
BZZZZZZTT

ALIYAH? WHAT ARE YOU--
I CAME TO...CHECK **IN** ON YOU. I HOPE THAT'S ALRIGHT...?

S-SURE.

BUT...?
SHH...

WE'VE EXTRACTED A SAMPLE OF NYX'S VENOM FROM JONAH'S BLOOD. IT'S BEING ANALYZED NOW.

I DON'T THINK A VAMPIRE WAS RESPONSIBLE FOR GLENDON'S DEATH, THOUGH SOMEONE TOOK GREAT PAINS TO MAKE IT LOOK THAT WAY.

ISN'T IT POSSIBLE A VAMPIRE--OR *ANYONE* FOR THAT MATTER--COULD HAVE PLANTED EVIDENCE THAT POINTS A FINGER AT ONE OF US GORGONS?

POSSIBLE, YES. BUT UNLIKELY. I THINK YOU KNOW THAT. I THINK YOU KNOW A GREAT MANY THINGS. AND I THINK YOU'RE READY TO SHARE THEM WITH ME, SO LET'S HAVE IT.

FEELS LIKE I'M BACK IN THE BOX WITH YOUR SON. A REAL CHIP OFF THE OLD BLOCK, ISN'T HE? YOU MUST BE VERY PROUD...

IT'S ***YOUR*** VENOM, ISN'T IT? IN GLENDON'S BLOOD? I CAN WAIT TO HEAR IT FROM DELPHIN, OR YOU CAN COME CLEAN RIGHT NOW.

YES, YES. IT'S MINE. BUT YOU HAVE TO UNDERSTAND...IT--NONE OF THIS WAS MY IDEA...
I'M LISTENING.

IT WAS DAMIEN. WE'D BEEN CARRYING ON FOR SOME TIME. IT WAS STUPID, BUT HE--THERE WAS JUST SOMETHING ABOUT HIM-- ANYWAY, IT WAS DAMIEN WHO KILLED GLENDON AND MADE ME TELL YOUR SON WHERE TO FIND HIM.

I DIDN'T KNOW MICHAEL WOULD BE-- ***COULD*** BE -- KILLED. YOU HAVE TO ***BELIEVE*** ME. WHEN I FOUND OUT WHAT HAPPENED, I WAS AFRAID TO SAY ANYTHING BECAUSE I WAS COMPLICIT.

BUT WHY? WHY SO MANY KILLINGS? AND WHY MICHAEL?
I DON'T KNOW! I DON'T KNOW ANYTHING ELSE. I WASN'T INVOLVED IN ANYTHING ELSE. IT-- I'M TELLING YOU IT WAS DAMIEN AND --!
AND? WHO ELSE WAS INVOLVED? MYA...!
NO. EVEN IF I TOLD YOU, YOU WOULDN'T BELIEVE ME. THAT'S WHY I'M GOING TO SHOW YOU.
DAMIEN'S SUPPOSED TO MEET HIS ACCOMPLICE TONIGHT, TO DISCUSS WHAT TO DO ABOUT YOUR SON. BUT YOU'LL HAVE TO PROMISE YOU'LL PROTECT ME. THERE'S NO TELLING WHAT THEY WOULD DO TO ME IF --!
JONAH'S IN DANGER?!
JONAH? JONAH, WHEN YOU GET THIS MESSAGE, COME MEET ME AS SOON AS POSSIBLE AT--
THE CLOISTERS MUSEUM.
AT THE CLOISTERS! LET TOBIAS AND DELPHIN KNOW, TOO. YOU WERE RIGHT ABOUT DAMIEN, SON, AND NOW WE'LL HAVE ALL THE PROOF WE NEED.

BUZZ BUZZ
BUZZ BUZZ

THE CLOISTERS MUSEUM, NEAR THE NORTHERN TIP OF MANHATTAN.
WE'RE EARLY.
WE CAN WAIT FOR THEM OVER THERE. OUT OF SIGHT.
AND YOU'RE SURE DAMIEN AND THIS... ACCOMPLICE OF HIS WILL SHOW?
OH, VERY SURE.
I'M SORRY, GABRIEL.
SKRRUNNCH
HUCCHH--?!?

RUNNING? REALLY?
THE CLOISTERS... A FITTING PLACE FOR A FORMER ARCHANGEL TO MEET HIS MAKER. WOULDN'T YOU AGREE?
WHO ARE YOU?
OH, MY GOD...
GOD? FAR FROM IT. JUST A RETURN TO THE WAY THINGS SHOULD BE. I'M JUST RESTORING SUPERNATURAL ORDER.
YOU MEAN SUPERNATURAL RULE. I'VE LIVED AS A HUMAN LONG ENOUGH TO KNOW PEACEFUL COEXISTENCE IS THE ONLY WAY.
MY SON IS THE EMBODIMENT OF THAT IDEAL. HE'LL KILL YOU FOR WHAT YOU'VE DONE.
CHUKKT

I was always kind of a nervous kid. Nightmares. Something under the bed. I remember my father telling me there was nothing to be afraid of. That there's no such thing as MONSTERS.
I believed him then. But now I know better.
TEMPUS
TEMPOR

Chapter Five

Written by:
Kevin McCarthy

Art by:
Paolo Pantalena

Colors by:
Bill Farmer

Letters by:
Troy Peteri

THE CLOISTERS, NYC.
ANOTHER DOUBLE IN RED ON THE BOARD. AN EX-COP IS BAD ENOUGH, BUT A U.S. CONGRESSWOMAN? THAT'S GOING TO BE PAPERWORK UP THE ASS.
SOME RESPECT, OKAY? DETECTIVE WRIGHT LOST HIS FATHER TONIGHT.
TEMPUS TEMPOR
FIRST ON THE SCENE FOUND THIS. NO MISTAKING WHOSE IT IS. IT'S LIKE A .357 CHEVY. HASN'T BEEN FIRED RECENTLY, BUT THE BLOOD RAISES QUESTIONS.
SO LET'S ASK THEM.
YOU OKAY TO TALK? WE RECOVERED YOUR SIDEARM. IT'S GOT SOME BLOOD ON IT.
...
BLOOD'S MINE. BUT THE GUN IS ALL YOURS. BADGE TOO, IF YOU WANT IT. I'M DONE BEING A COP. TRYING TO BE SOME KIND OF AN...ANGEL...
?
THAT'S THE GRIEF TALKING. MAYBE YOU SHOULD TALK TO SOMEBODY? BEEN THROUGH HELL THE PAST FEW WEEKS.
AND YOUR SAFETY'S NOW AN ISSUE. YOU COULD BE NEXT ON THE KILLER'S LIST, SO WE'RE PUTTING A DETAIL ON YOU.
DO WHAT YOU'VE GOT TO DO.
TEMPUS TEMPOR
And I'll do what I'VE got to do.

THE TRUMP BUILDING, 40 WALL STREET, NYC.

"Tempus Temporis." Four years at Cardinal Hayes taught me enough Latin to know it means "Epoch." A message meant for me? A warning?

I should've just done this from the beginning.

Why am I not surprised that a demon like Damien would hide in plain sight in the financial district?

YOU LADIES MIGHT WANT TO TAKE LUNCH. I'M HERE TO KILL YOUR BOSS.

HOW IS YOUR INVESTIGATION COMING ALONG, DETECTIVE?
I KNOW YOU KILLED MY FATHER. BUT SINCE I CAN'T PROVE IT, I'M GOING TO BEAT A CONFESSION OUT OF YOU, OLD SCHOOL.
BITCHES, LEAVE.

YOU SHOULDN'T BE HERE. WE'RE DANGEROUSLY CLOSE TO VIOLATING THE TOURNAMENT RULES.
MUCH AS I WANT TO KILL YOU RIGHT NOW, I WON'T DO ANYTHING THAT COULD JEOPARDIZE MY SHOT AT FINALLY WINNING EPOCH.

FUCK EPOCH!
KRESSGH
I'M GUESSING THAT VASE WAS WORTH MORE TO ME THAN YOU WERE WORTH TO YOUR OLD MAN. IS *THAT* WHY YOU'RE SO UPSET?
NNNGH!
I MAY NOT BE ABLE TO ATTACK YOU. BUT I *AM* ALLOWED TO DEFEND MYSELF.
OWW--!
IF I *DID* KILL YOUR FATHER, I IMAGINE HE LOOKED MUCH LIKE YOU DO NOW. HELPLESS. AFRAID.
IF I *DID* KILL YOUR FATHER--AND I'M NOT ADMITTING ANYTHING HERE--HE PROBABLY PISSED HIMSELF LIKE THE PATHETIC OLD MAN HE BECAME.
AND IF I *HAD* KILLED MICHAEL-- HYPOTHETICALLY-- I'LL BET THE LOOK OF DISAPPOINTMENT WHEN HE REALIZED YOU'D FAILED HIM AS A PARTNER WAS FUCKING *PRICELESS*.

IT WOULD BE SOOOOO EASY TO BURN YOU TO ASH RIGHT NOW. ALMOST WORTH FORFEITING THE TOURNAMENT.
DO IT.
GLADLY. BUT NOT HERE.
NOT LIKE THIS.
I WANT EVERY SUPERNATURAL TO WITNESS WHEN I END THE ARCHANGEL BLOODLINE, AND ASSUME CONTROL OF THE COUNCIL.
TCNN

It's going to happen just like he says. It'll mean the end of days. For humanity, anyway.

AND I WAS SUPPOSED TO SAVE THE WORLD? WHAT A *JOKE.* I COULDN'T EVEN SAVE MICHAEL. OR DAD...

eritatis

MY GOD. DAD...YOU WERE FINALLY BACK IN MY LIFE AGAIN, AND...AND...

DAMMIT!

IT'S OKAY, FELLAS. BAD MARKET DAY. I WAS JUST LEAVING.
I don't know what to do.
It doesn't matter anymore.

ROOSEVELT HOSPITAL AMBULANCE BAY.

ALIYAH...?

THEY MAKE US DO OUR OWN MAINTENANCE HERE. CAN YOU BELIEVE THAT?

DOES THE DEPARTMENT MAKE ***YOU*** CHANGE THE OIL ON YOUR UNMARKED -- WHAT'S WRONG?

MY FATHER'S DEAD. ***KILLED.*** ALONG WITH MY INFORMANT. AND MY CASE.

WHAT--?!

I JUST CAME BY TO TELL YOU THAT I'M FINISHED. WITH ***EPOCH.*** WITH ***ALL*** OF IT...

YOU CAN'T ***MEAN*** THAT! I KNOW YOU AND GABRIEL WERE JUST BEGINNING TO...
SO YOU'RE JUST GOING TO GIVE UP? AND LET DAMIEN GET AWAY WITH HIS MURDER? AND ***MICHAEL'S?***
JUST...BEFORE YOU DECIDE ANYTHING, COME WITH ME. I WANT TO SHOW YOU SOMETHING.

EVERYBODY HERE... THEY'RE SUPERNATURAL, RIGHT?
THE MAJORITY ARE. WE'VE GOTTEN VERY GOOD AT BLENDING IN WITH THE HUMAN POPULACE OVER THE YEARS.
BUT MORE THAN THAT, WE'VE FINALLY ACHIEVED PEACEFUL COEXISTENCE.
AND IF THE COUNCIL FALLS INTO THE WRONG HANDS, BLAH BLAH BLAH, THE END OF THE WORLD AS WE KNOW IT? I DON'T GIVE A SHIT ANYMORE. I JUST WANT REVENGE.
BUT I CAN'T BEAT DAMIEN. I'VE TRIED.
I'M TELLING YOU, YOU CAN BEAT HIM. YOU HAVE TO! OR MICHAEL'S AND YOUR FATHER'S DEATHS WILL HAVE BEEN FOR NOTHING.
THEY SAW SOMETHING IN YOU. LIKE I DO.
WHATEVER. FIRST YOU'RE ALL "SHH" AND PUTTING THE MOVES ON ME. THEN YOU JUST DISAPPEAR, ACTING LIKE NOTHING HAPPENED.
THAT--THAT WAS A MISTAKE. GABRIEL'S DEATH SO SOON AFTER MICHAEL'S IS--I CAN'T BEGIN TO IMAGINE HOW YOU MUST FEEL. BUT YOU'LL HAVE TO KEEP YOUR EMOTIONS IN CHECK.
IF THAT'S WHAT BEING AN ARCHANGEL MEANS, THEN I'M NOT SURE I WANT ANY PART OF IT.
WHAT DO YOU WANT? CALL US A MISTAKE, BUT IF YOU'RE SO IN CONTROL, HOW DID WE HAPPEN IN THE FIRST PLACE?
THERE'S NO MISTAKING WHAT I FEEL FOR YOU, JONAH. BUT WE CAN'T--I WON'T LET IT GET IN THE WAY OF WHAT YOU NEED TO DO.

LATER, IN THE ZARQA RIVER VALLEY, JORDAN.

I pull myself together long enough to attend an Order of Angels funeral service for Michael.

I should be up there with them, but I'm not ANGEL enough to have wings.

And wasn't MAN enough to have prevented this from happening in the first place.

YOU KNOW, NOT FAR FROM HERE, A MAN NAMED JACOB WRESTLED ONE OF US AND IT MADE ALL THE PAPERS.

I WISH I KNEW HOW HE DID IT. HOW HE WAS ABLE TO HOLD HIS OWN AGAINST AN UNBEATABLE OPPONENT.

BY HAVING ***FAITH.*** MAYBE YOURS WAS LOST WITH MICHAEL AND GABRIEL. BUT I HAVE FAITH IN ***YOU.*** SO DOES ***ALIYAH.*** WE WANTED YOU AS OUR CHAMPION FOR YOUR ***SPIRIT*** AS MUCH AS FOR YOUR LINEAGE.

BLOOD IS BLOOD, BUT THE ***FIRE*** WITHIN YOU IS WHAT WILL WIN OVER ***ANY*** OPPONENT. IT BURNS HOTTER THAN ANYTHING

THOUGH I LACK THIS FIRE MYSELF, I CAN RECOGNIZE IT IN OTHERS. MICHAEL HAD IT. YOUR FATHER HAD IT. AND SO DO YOU.

UNTIL YOU CAN PROVE IT TO YOURSELF, YOU MUST HAVE FAITH AS WELL.

"FAITH," HUH? DOES THAT MEAN MICHAEL AND MY FATHER ARE LOOKING DOWN ON US FROM HEAVEN, OR IS THAT JUST BULLSHIT?
THERE IS AN AFTERLIFE. DOES IT EASE YOUR MIND TO KNOW YOUR LOVED ONES ARE AT PEACE AND IN SOME BETTER PLACE?
NO. I JUST WANT THEM TO WATCH WHEN I KILL THE MOTHERFUCKER WHO PUT THEM THERE.
MIDTOWN MANHATTAN.
The brass sprung for this since Pop "died heroically while protecting a Congresswoman."
At least, that's the way they wrote it up.
I think the old man would've preferred this to a flight of angels.

Now I have to make MINE.
Wheelock and Williams were already here.
Super must've let them in, because I took the keys off my old man when I found him.
I was looking for something else, but he didn't have it on him. I hope it's here.
St. Michael. Patron saint of police officers. And, WARRIORS.
Maybe some faith would do me good.

Next, I have to face the music before the Council. I'd love to tell them I've already FOUND their supernatural serial killer...
...but without hard evidence, it's just my word against Damien's.
And my word doesn't carry any weight in this room.
WELL, DETECTIVE, THUS FAR, YOUR INVESTIGATION HAS YIELDED ONLY TWO MORE DEATHS -- INCLUDING A RESPECTED MEMBER OF THIS COUNCIL!
HOW IS ANY OF THAT HIS FAULT? HAVE YOU DEMONS DONE ANYTHING TO HELP STOP THE KILLINGS? OR ARE YOU TOO CONSUMED WITH WINNING EPOCH?
HOW DARE YOU SIDE WITH A HUMAN AGAINST ONE OF OUR OWN? HAS ESTRUS BLINDED YOU TO THE FACT THAT ALL OUR TROUBLES BEGAN WHEN HE SHOWED UP?
YES! AND HOW COULD HE END UP IN THE FINALS OF EPOCH WITHOUT HAVING CHEATED? I SAY WE VOID THIS TOURNAMENT AND BEGIN AGAIN!
BECAUSE YOUR LUNA LOST TO GRIM IN THE FIRST ROUND? AND MY DAMIEN IS ONE STEP AWAY FROM ULTIMATE VICTORY?
Things are already getting out of hand. The Council will fall apart without the right leader. I can see that now.

Even though I have almost no shot, I've got to do everything I can to make sure Damien doesn't win.
So much blood and violence, to prevent yet more blood and violence.
EPOCH isn't just a necessary evil; it's vital to the survival of both the human and supernatural races.
Aliyah has trained me. Michael inspired me. And my father showed me what sacrifices must be made in order to do what's right.
It's all up to ME, now.

THE COLOSSEUM, ROME, ITALY.
Or else, I'll be the latest in a very long line of VICTIMS that have been thrown to the lions here.
I WENT EASY ON YOU LAST TIME, DETECTIVE! THIS TIME, THERE'LL BE NOTHING LEFT OF YOU TO HEAL YOURSELF WITH.

BRUKK
VUH!
KLUDD
VRAH--!
BAM
PATHETIC.
IT'S PROBABLY FOR THE BEST THAT YOUR FATHER-- AND MICHAEL--AREN'T HERE TO SEE WHAT AN EMBARRASSING "LEGACY" THEY'VE LEFT BEHIND.
GNAH!
He's right. I'm getting my ass handed to me. Again.
Time to start acting like the archangel I'm supposed to be.

SPTT.
ROARR!
HSTT.
KRAK
GRAH!
HAAHH!
K-BRUKT
DEJA VU, EH, DETECTIVE? SHOULD'VE KNOWN YOU WOULDN'T FIGHT WITH ANY HEART TONIGHT...
...I PUNCHED IT OUT OF YOUR CHEST THE NIGHT I KILLED MICHAEL!

I'm BURNING!
It's Aliyah's Fire Test all over again. The one I FAILED...
Just like NOW. It's over. I'm finished!
AH-HA-HA-HA-HA-HAH!
The pain is... excruciating, just like before. But something's different, like, I'm at peace with it all. Dying isn't...so bad...
Wait... what's--?
VA-VAM

I think I understand now.
The Fire Test, the Dome...I was never in enough danger to trigger my forced evolution into an ARCHANGEL.
Even the hole in my chest was recoverable from just my dormant archangel DNA. But being utterly destroyed by fire?
I had to DIE so I could be reborn...
THINK I GIVE A FUCK? THINK THIS *CHANGES* ANYTHING?
I'LL KILL YOU AS MANY TIMES AS I HAVE TO!
HNNNGH!
SMACH

POLLICE VERSO!
THE CROWD WANTS YOU DEAD. THAT MAKES IT UNANIMOUS.
BUT FIRST, YOU'RE GOING TO TELL ME WHO YOU'RE WORKING WITH. NO WAY YOU DID THIS ALL ON YOUR OWN. IS IT LILITH? WHO?
I'LL NEVER TELL! AND I WON'T TAP OUT. I'LL FORCE YOUR HAND. BUT IF YOU KILL ME, YOU'LL NEVER KNOW THE TRUTH.
I DON'T HAVE TO KILL YOU. YOU'RE BEATEN. IT'S OVER.
DON'T BE SO SURE--!
NYAAGH!
WHAM
What an incredible feeling. This is a timeless moment. It could be ten thousand years ago, and it would be no different.
And now I am a part of it.

Then, the moment passes. And it's back to life as usual. We supernaturals have to blend in, you know.

For me, that means going back to work. Officially, Glendon et al. goes down as cold.

Unofficially, I'm still working the case.

And no, I didn't appoint myself head of the Council. I'm not Michael. Frankly, neither is TOBIAS.
He didn't even WANT the job at first, but I talked him into it.

He, in turn, appointed ME to be a sort of supernatural detective, to continue investigating the unsolved murders.
And whatever OTHER shady shit these maniacs get into.

To my surprise, none of the Council members objected. Not even Aliyah, the new leader of the Order of Angels.

It's over between us. Better that way. Despite our feelings, it wasn't right betraying Tobias like that. But he'll never know anything happened.
It KILLS me that I never discovered who Damien was working with. And that the SWORD is still out there...
Maybe Damien would've eventually confessed, who knows? Tobias says not to beat myself up about it.
He's helped me find closure with everything that's happened. He's good like that. A gentle and caring soul.
I know he'll make it his mission to steer the supernaturals towards peaceful coexistence with each other, and mankind.

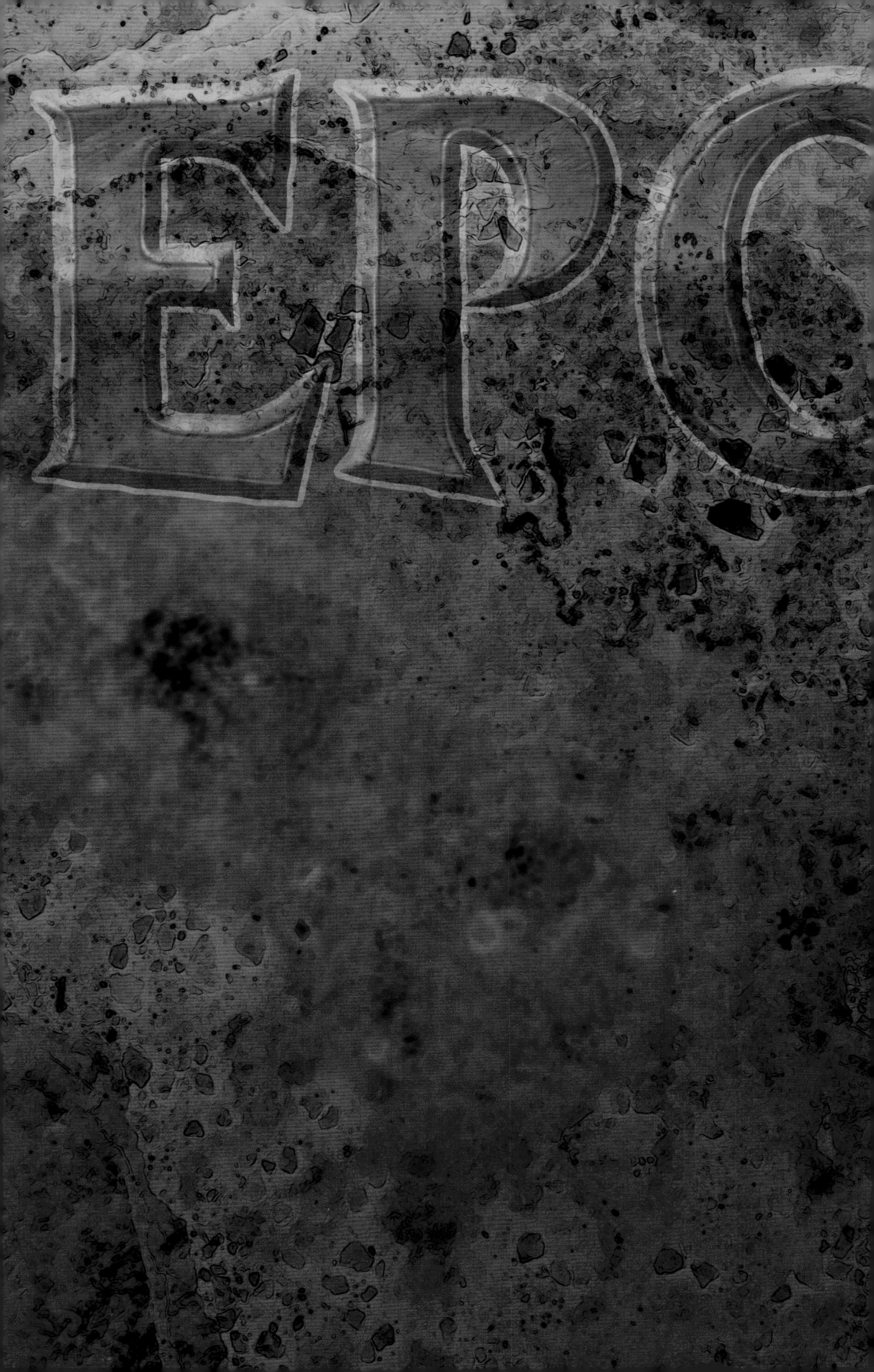

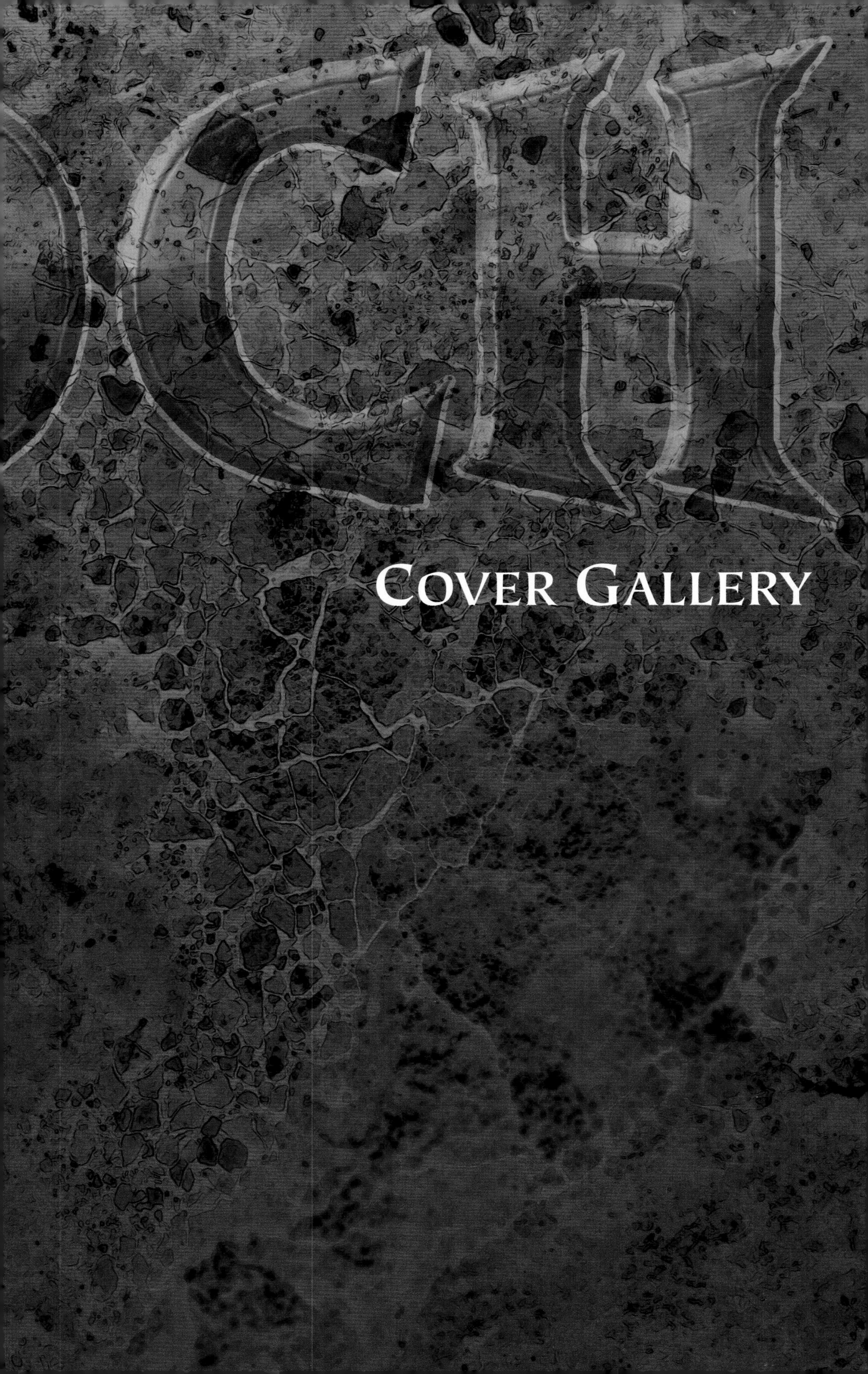

Cover Gallery

Epoch issue #1 Cover A
art by: **Paolo Pantalena & Paolo Barbieri**

Epoch issue #1 Cover B San Diego Comic Con Exclusive
art by: Paolo Pantalena

Epoch issue #2 Cover

art by: **Paolo Pantalena & Paolo Barbieri**

Epoch issue #3 Cover
art by: Paolo Pantalena & Bill Farmer

Epoch issue #4 Cover Pencils

art by: **Paolo Pantalena**

Epoch issue #4 Cover
art by: Paolo Pantalena & Bill Farmer
FARMER

Epoch issue #5 Cover

art by: **Paolo Pantalena & Bill Farmer**

The Species of... EPOCH

-ANGELS-

Once upon a time, there were millions of Angels, but a bloody civil war led them to the brink of extinction. Cut off from God's guidance, the few that were left were forced to blend in with mankind. Under Michael's leadership, Angels watched over man and the Earth, keeping both in balance for God. Blessed with immortality and dedicated to the protection of humanity, they became modern-day society's first responders and guardians (i.e., doctors, policemen, firemen, paramedics, etc.).

Traditionally, most Angels are not warriors. In fact, they are the last ones to involve themselves in a war. This being said, Archangels are supreme fighters, able to defeat any species in one-on-one combat. However, their number have dwindled over time and the Archangel Michael is the last of his kind.

Archangels prefer the fighting styles of Jeet Kune Do and Aikido. They are balanced and cerebral fighters: strong, fast, and intelligent. They believe every attack exposes a weakness, thereby offering a perfect counter-attack. When drawn into a fight, they quickly analyze an opponent, determine his/her weakness and attack it quickly and decisively. They are neither the fastest nor strongest, but they have few deficiencies. The irony of the Archangel's benevolent existence is that they, in fact, are the perfect fighters. Angels can fly, but rarely do so to prevent drawing attention. An Angel's wings are his/her source of power, but they keep them hidden so they can navigate our world without raising suspicion.

-DEMONS-

Demons are amongst the most mythical and storied creatures inhabiting our world. Eons ago, they were defeated in the Great War against the Angels, banned from heaven, securing their ill-fated fortune as lost-Angels. They are ambitious, passionate, and powerful. They're rife with lust and desire and excel in any high-stakes, fast-paced lifestyle that gets their adrenaline pumping. They are ruthless lawyers, unstoppable athletes, and overzealous Midtown powerbrokers.

Seemingly human, Demons are masters of Pyrokinesis – the ability to excite and speed up atoms, increasing their thermal energy until they ignite. With this great power, they can set objects aflame, throw fiery projectiles, and even light themselves on fire. Demons burn incredibly hot, and each has their own proprietary color of flame (i.e., red, yellow, orange, blue, etc.). In hand-to-hand combat, they utilize their fiery abilities to singe, burn, and torment their opponent until submission or death. The hotter they burn, the faster they become. And, the faster they become, the hotter they burn. It's a vicious cycle. Despite these great powers, Demons do have a weakness – they don't possess superhuman strength. Only the super-quick, super-strong, and super-determined stand a chance.

Demons use Jiu-jitsu as their primary fighting style. They keep their opponents at bay with their fiery projectiles...until the fight turns to close-quarters. Once this happens, their fighting becomes methodical. They wear down their opponents and prey on their impatience. Once a Demon locks up their aggressor, they bring the wrath of hell – a slow excruciating torture that few opponents can escape.

-VAMPIRES-

Vampires are the dark and mysterious beings of the Supernatural world. Being nocturnal creatures, they have naturally integrated themselves into all things related to nightlife. From nightclubs to bars and burlesque shows to sex clubs, Vampires find themselves most at home feeding off of the energy of the night. Vampires are thrill seekers and adrenaline junkies who love the danger of racing the newest motorcycles and flashy sports cars and are attracted to anything that makes the blood flow... especially humans. They stay in close proximity, feeding off of our human energy.

In battle, they are fierce warriors and difficult to defeat. They possess superhuman strength but are not as strong as Werewolves or Trolls. They are agile, elusive, wily, and are able to absorb blows, feeding off of the energy of their opponent. Their fighting style is similar to that of Capoeira mixed with Gymnastics. Their fights are dictated by a rhythm. If they dictate the rhythm, they win. If their

-WEREWOLVES-

Once upon a time, there were millions of Angels, but a Werewolves are the Supernatural world's version of organized crime – the mafia. They run the docks, construction zones, waste management, taxi alliances, shipping, and other mafia-associated businesses. Werewolves are street-smart and rely on intimidation and brute strength to accomplish most of their goals. Werewolves have had one of the hardest adjustments going underground. Werewolves have a difficult time keeping their primal instincts in check, and as passionate beings it's easy to push them over the limit.

In battle, Werewolves are ferocious fighters who depend on their strength and agility to out-muscle and overwhelm an opponent. Their berserker style attacks are akin to the mauling of an angry grizzly bear. They use the quick strike, close-quarter styles of Muay Thai Boxing and Krav Maga to their advantage, but they naturally lack stamina. Their key to victory is evading an opponent's attack in

-TROLLS-

Trolls are the most mysterious of all Supernatural beings. Born of the earth, no one knows how they are created or from who or where they came. A race of all males, they are short-tempered and reclusive but renowned for their wisdom and intelligence. Their private lifestyle and superior intelligence makes them ideal museum curators, inventors, librarians, and scientists. Though reclusive, they will band together to defend their species. They live long, quiet lives of solitude, often dedicated to a single pursuit, like most of the world's greatest scientific discoveries.

In battle, Trolls have the best defensive abilities of all Supernatural creatures. They have thick, leathery skin that is tough and hardened. Using a combination of Heavyweight Boxing and Old School Pro Wrestling, Trolls wear an opponent down to the point of exhaustion. And, when they do, they have a powerful knock-out blow. Trolls are highly subversive and antagonistic in battle. They use their superior intelligence to psychologically overpower an opponent. But, despite all their strengths, Trolls do have weaknesses. They are slow, lacking mobility and agility. And, they have a limited offensive arsenal. Trolls will take the brunt of an offensive attack, frustrating their opponents, drawing them in closer and waiting for the perfect moment to unleash a knockout punch. Like Achilles, an opponent must find each Troll's weakness. And, when they do, victory can be theirs.

-WARLOCKS-

Witches and Warlocks have been living amongst humankind since the dawn of time...but in very small numbers. Always feared for their seemingly devilish capabilities, they've been persecuted and hunted. In the Middle Ages and recent centuries, they've been tracked and burned at the stake, resulting in a depletion of their numbers. In reality, they're not all that different from us. But, their Wican DNA enables them master Telekinesis and control the elements through harnessing the energy of their surrounding environment. Today, as captains of industry, Wicans blend in with high society, much like the modern day Rockefellers, Carnegies, and Mellons. But, they've cloaked their Wican abilities from the watchful eyes of those around them.

In battle, Wicans utilize their abilities and magic to throw objects across the room, levitate, and control the elements around them. They can also distort their attacker's visual perception in order to gain an advantage. Conversely, their weakness is the fact that they're basically human, so they have to keep their opponents at a distance and use the elements around them to defend themselves. While they play with the laws of physics, they have no extraordinary healing power. So if they're mortally wounded, they will die much like any other human.

The Wican fighting style is Kung Fu. Like Wican, Kung Fu harnesses the energy of the surrounding environment to create a tactical advantage when fighting an opponent. There is never a single approach to victory; they allow the situation to dictate the correct course of action.

-GORGONS-

Gorgons are a vicious race of female serpentines with sharp fangs, snake tongue, impenetrable scaly skin, and a dragon-like tail. They are descendents of Medusa, however they do not possess Medusa's ability to turn man into stone. Gorgons are chameleons with the ability to shape-shift and assume various human forms (they appear human to mankind). They are the perfect politicians, strategists, and excel anywhere that duplicity is an asset.

In battle, Gorgons are as elusive and deadly as a poisonous snake. They have tough exteriors made of impenetrable scales. They are not as strong as Trolls defensively but have amazing defensive and regenerative abilities. Gorgons' fighting style is Ninjutsu, a combination of stealth and deception. They maneuver quickly around an opponent and can attack with all five limbs. Much like snakes and other venomous creatures, Gorgons can bite their enemies and induce paralysis. A Gorgon's bite is deadly to humans and paralytic to Supernatural beings. Gorgons can regenerate their limbs if severed from their bodies. It is not uncommon for a Gorgon to feign injury. In doing so, they are able to lure in an opponent, causing them to let down their guard. In an instant, they strike, incapacitating their victim and leaving them helpless in the ring. Death by decapitation is the

-BANSHEES-

Banshees are an all-female race of fairy-like beings. They are mesmerizingly beautiful and extremely lethal. They've found their niche in society as models, singers, entertainers, and assassins. Along with their angelic voices, Banshees are equipped with retractable razor-sharp and needle-thin fingernails. They have extensive knowledge of the human physiology and use this to their advantage and understand the best places to strike and quickly incapacitate their opponent. They can puncture someone's artery creating a wound so small that the victim doesn't notice until it is too late. Additionally, they have the power to levitate, but only themselves.

Other than their lethal fingernails and levitation abilities, Banshees are basically human (albeit extraordinarily attractive), and therefore very susceptible to blows. In battle, they maintain distance from their opponent and play to their quick-strike abilities. They are at the disadvantage in a close-quarters fight, especially with a stronger, more powerful opponent. They always attempt to strike first and end the fight as quickly as possible. A Banshee's fighting style is Karate, specifically loaded with high-flying, acrobatic aerial attacks. Because of their fragile physical attributes, they're all offense and no defense.

-ANGELS-

Head of the Supernatural Council:
ARCHANGEL MICHAEL

During the Dark Ages, Michael won EPOCH to bring order to the world of Supernaturals, securing their future. In victory, he appointed himself the head of the Supernatural Council – a decision that enabled Supernaturals to coexist with humans for a thousand years. Today, Michael is a detective. He's been investigating the recent deaths of both humans and Supernaturals. Through his keen detective work, he discovers a conspiracy at hand...the harbinger of a coming war. The conspiracy runs deep within the Supernaturals, and Michael is dead-set on uncovering the puppeteer pulling the strings!

Human/Archangel:
JONAH BISHOP

Our reluctant hero, Jonah Bishop, is an NYPD detective and Michael's partner. When Michael is brutally killed, Jonah makes it his mission to find his murderer and ultimately unveil the truth behind his life and heritage. You see, Jonah's human mother died during childbirth. Consequently, he was raised by his reclusive father, Gabriel – a former Angel. But, Gabriel never revealed this secret, yet Jonah followed in his father's footsteps and joined the police force where he quickly rose to detective. Through this adventure, Jonah will learn the truth about his father and begin to understand the tragic tale that has become his father's life. He will also learn of his true calling – becoming the last Archangel. He is the last of his kind, and he must train to assume his role as a warrior Angel. Jonah will become his peoples' champion and find a sense of belonging for the first time in his life.

Human:
GABRIEL/GABE BISHOP
(Former Archangel)

An Archangel like Michael, Gabriel was once his protégé. He was equally as impressive in battle (some say better) and was destined to succeed him some day as the leader of the Supernatural Council and head of the Angel Order. Unexpectedly, he fell in love with a human woman, which is forbidden for Angels, and chose her over the Angel Order. A mortal life of love proved to be even shorter than he had imagined when a cruel twist of fate robbed him of his one true love – his wife – when she died in childbirth. Taking the name of Gabe Bishop, he lived his mortal life in solitude, mourning her death, raising their son Jonah and waiting for God's mercy to allow him to reunite with his true love in the afterlife. Today, Gabe Bishop is a run-down, ex-cop, 60's, with few friends and few joys in this life. A shadow of his former, proud-warrior self, he is given new purpose when he learns of Michael's murder.

Council Member:
TOBIAS

While Michael sat at the head of the Supernatural Council, Tobias was appointed to represent the Angel Order. He was Michael's close friend, most recent protégé and served as his chief advisor. Before the time of man, Tobias fell in love with Aliyah. At first, she was not receptive to his advances but his persistence wore her down, and she eventually married him. Today their marriage has clearly transformed from a once passionate affair into a partnership based more on trust and mutual respect. But, while she remains a devoted wife, he is careful to conceal the fact that he frequently takes lovers to quench his sexual appetite. Tobias is meticulous in his every action: calm, calculating, and far more rational than his hot-tempered and emotional wife. Tobias is not an Archangel, and realizes that he cannot step in for Michael in battle – he must find a warrior to represent his people.

Angel:
ALIYAH

A paramedic in human form, Aliyah is a true believer in the principles of the Angel Order and their purpose as the world's guardians. She is emotional and ruled by her heart. Like Tobias, when Michael dies, she becomes a leader of her people. At first, she is against bringing Jonah into the Angel Order and looks down on Gabriel for his decision to leave the Angels for a human. But, eventually, she recognizes that she is a lot more like Gabriel than she had originally thought. Reluctantly, she agrees to help train Jonah for EPOCH. She feels a strange and uncontrollable connection to Jonah…she tries to fight her feelings for the sake of her marriage but eventually may give in to her desires.

-DEMONS-

Warrior: DAMIAN

A Corporate Raider, Damian is the Gordon Gecko of the powerbroker world. Ultra-aggressive. Ultra competitive. Fast cars, beautiful women, and a staggering drug habit consume him, defining the life of this overzealous bachelor in the ultimate fast lane. But, there's a method to Damian's madness. Every inch of him detests humanity. He believes Supernaturals should rule over mankind, and he's waiting for his moment to bring his wrath to the human world.

Council Member: LILITH

LILITH is Creation's first ex-wife. She hosts a sharp wit and a keen intellect. Throughout history, she's dominated numerous high-powered leadership positions. Today, she's the highest-ranking NYC defense attorney. She has a penchant for winning all the highest-profile cases, especially when a Supernatural is involved. Single, she looks to be in her 50's, and is incredibly well connected in the legal community where she's considered an unstoppable force. She's well-regarded by humans, but knows their place in her society.

-VAMPIRES-

Council Member: *CYRUS*

Cyrus was an African slave captured by the Egyptians during the rule of Ramesses 2nd (aka Ramesses the Great) and forced to serve as a pyramid builder. He caught the eye of the Pharaoh's wife and soon became her lover. Their relationship lasted for years, but the Pharaoh discovered the secret lovers and tried to have Cyrus executed. To save his life, she smuggled him out of Egypt with a band of gypsy traders. He spent a few years working as a trader, traveling throughout the world. One night, at a gypsy caravan festival, he fell for the wrong woman, a gypsy Vampire. She ultimately turned him. Since then, he has traveled the world and taken many lovers. As the oldest surviving Vampire, he is the head of his order. He runs a nightclub empire and is the undisputed king of nightlife in New York.

Warrior: RAFAEL

Born a commoner in the city of Tenochtitlan, Rafael was promoted and rose to the highest rank of Aztec nobility, becoming the greatest warrior under emperors Montezuma I & II. He helped the Aztec Empire spread its domain by conquering neighboring lands, winning their riches, and collecting bodies to sacrifice to the gods. He defended the great Aztec Empire from the Spanish Conquistadors (i.e., Cortez, etc.) and was ultimately turned by Cyrus while awaiting his death as a Spanish prisoner.

-WEREWOLVES-

Council Member:
RASPUTIN

Many legends have been told about the Mad Monk, Rasputin, but none were true. The truth is that Grigori Rasputin came from a long line of Russian Werewolves believed to originate from the Siberian countryside. During the late 19th Century, he rose to power as chief advisor and religious council to the Czar and Czarina. The murder of Rasputin has become legend, some of it invented by the very men who killed him, which is why it becomes difficult to discern exactly what happened. In short, he was lured into a trap by the Prince and Grand Duke and managed to survive poisoning, multiple stab wounds, and a gunshot before finally dying. He was buried, but the body disappeared, which was unexplainable until we realize that Rasputin was a powerful Werewolf and managed to take advantage of this attempted murder to go underground just in time to avoid the people's revolution, suffering the same fate as the Czars...a slow, painful death. Today, he is the head of the Werewolf Order, a Hoffa-esque leader who is a ticking time bomb waiting to explode. The question remains: is he a madman or genius?

Warrrior: LUNA

Luna was the daughter of a French Buccaneer during the 17th Century, who traveled with her father on his adventures throughout the Caribbean. Living a pirate's life with her swashbuckling father, she grew up to be a fearsome fighter. While docked in the port city of Tortuga on her 21st birthday, she was attacked by a rival band of pirates. Screaming for help, no help would come, and suddenly her fear turned to rage, and her rage unleashed a secret that had laid dormant in her family's DNA...LUNA was a Werewolf. When her father's crew learned the truth, they thought she had been bewitched, killed her father (suspecting him of the same) and branded her with the mark of the Fleur-de-lis (mark of a criminal). They attempted to cast her overboard, but her rage once again allowed her to transform into the Werewolf, and she slaughtered the men painting the boat with their mutinous blood. Seemingly alone, she wandered the earth for years before finally discovering the Werewolf Order. She found a new father figure in Rasputin. Today, she is the ultimate union enforcer.

-TROLLS-

Warrior:
GRIM

Like Delphin, Grim was born of the earth, specifically from the bloody battlefields once conquered by the great Ghengis Khan. Like all Trolls, Grim is both intelligent and short-tempered, but he was imbued with the skills of a stout warrior. Tough to the core, he can wear down an opponent with his wit and shear strength, making him a formidable opponent for any Supernatural.

Council Member:
DELPHIN

Delphin, like all Trolls, was born of the earth. Reclusive since a very young age, he found his way in the recessed classrooms and laboratories of the world's greatest institutions. There's Mensa smart...and then there is off-the-charts Troll smart, which plays perfectly into Delphin's eremitic life. He comes from a long line of brilliant scientists, having made some of the world's greatest discoveries. He is as short-tempered as he is smart, but he has learned to channel his anger into his work. Delphin is a Supernatural forensic expert and will aid Jonah and Gabriel in their investigation of Supernatural deaths.

-WARLOCKS-

Warrior:
GRIFFIN

Young, cool, and super ambitious. Griffin is a masterful Warlock for his young age, but he doesn't subscribe to the adages of old. He's not going to pay his dues to seize the power he believes he deserves. Unlike Bianca's mild disdain for mankind, Griffin harbors a vengeful hatred. But, this comes as no surprise to a Wican orphan whose London-born parents were brutally murdered by the notorious Cray Brothers.

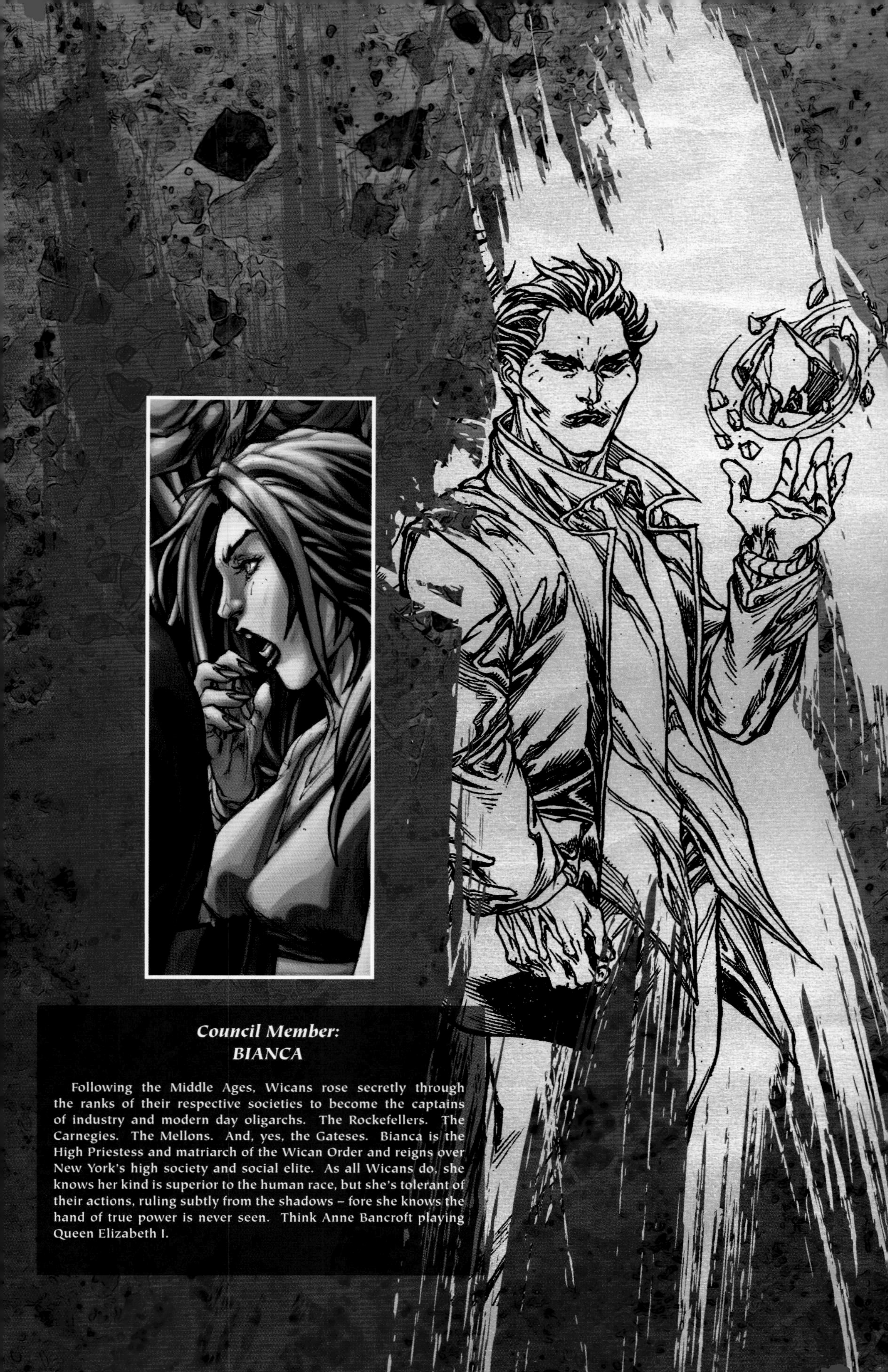

Council Member:
BIANCA

Following the Middle Ages, Wicans rose secretly through the ranks of their respective societies to become the captains of industry and modern day oligarchs. The Rockefellers. The Carnegies. The Mellons. And, yes, the Gateses. Bianca is the High Priestess and matriarch of the Wican Order and reigns over New York's high society and social elite. As all Wicans do, she knows her kind is superior to the human race, but she's tolerant of their actions, ruling subtly from the shadows – fore she knows the hand of true power is never seen. Think Anne Bancroft playing Queen Elizabeth I.

-GORGONS-

WARRIOR: NYX

Said to be a distant relative of the raped Medusa, Nyx comes from a long bloodline of female warriors in the image of Ahhotep, Joan of Arc, and Zenobia. Nyx lives her life where she likes it – in the shadows. At the top of her game, she plays the infallible "fixer" to countless corrupt politicians, and her deft hand for political cover-up is only outmatched by her skills as a slivering fighter in the ring.

Council Member:
MYA

Gorgons, like Mya, have been around since the dawn of time and walk the line between good and evil. On one hand, Gorgons have been the world's most influential and beneficent women. On the other, Gorgons have spawned history's worst, like Queen Mary I (i.e., Bloody Mary) and Irma Grese (the "Bitch of Belsen"), the unscrupulous female guard at concentration camps in Ravensbruck, Auschwitz, and Bergen-Belsen. Mya is of this lineage. With great deceit, Mya has risen through the ranks, becoming one of New York's most celebrated and politically charged congresswomen. She's a strong-minded mother of devilishly-darling, quintuple Gorgon girls. They are her heritage, and she is paving the political highway, in both this and the Supernatural world, for their eventual rise to power.

-BANSHEES-

Council Member: GISELLE

Giselle is the smoking-hot queen of the Banshees. Her mother was the last Council representative (as was her grandmother and all of her ancestors) and she was specifically bred and raised to assume this role for the Banshee Order. She may only be in her mid 20's, but Giselle has the benefits of thousands of years of ancestry, breeding queen after queen, refining their abilities to lead with each generation. She must conceive a child to complete her duties as queen and begin training the next generation of the Banshee leaders.

Warrior: SLOAN

Sloan (Early 20's) is everything a Banshee should be: graceful, beautiful, sophisticated, and lethal in every sense of the word. Her beauty and alluring nature allows her to gain access to the most inaccessible targets in the world, and this makes her a most terrifying and lethal assassin. She slips into many different roles in order to get close to her mark – a waitress, singer, model, etc. – and lets her gorgeous exterior mask her dark and mysterious interior. Losing her mother at an early age forced her to grow up very quickly. She fended for herself, teaching her to fight and use her abilities as effectively as possible. Being a Banshee, she has an impeccable knowledge of the human physiology, making her the ultimate assassin. She spends her regular nights as a lounge singer at a local club where her sultry voice enchants the minds and hearts of unsuspecting patrons, totally oblivious to the fact that they're watching an utterly lethal operator.

Sketch Gallery

Before Paolo Pantalena was determined to be the artist best suited for Epoch, Top Cow alumni Eric 'eBas' Basaldua was commissioned to complete character designs and a handful of test pages for the series. Although Epoch evolved toward a different aesthetic from the samples Eric provided, his early sketches had a hand in developing the world of Epoch.

Top Cow proudly presents this sneak peek into the sketchbook of Eric Basaldua as a rare glimpse into viewing the creative process that goes into the front-end world building of a brand new comic book property.

Michael,
Head of Supernatural Council

JONAS

Jonah,
half human half angel

ALIYAH = UNDERWORLD
Aliyah,
Angel and wife of
Tobias
TOBIAS = UNDERWORLD
Tobias,
Angel and future
Supernatual Council
Leader
Gabriel/Gabe Bishop,
Human, once an Angel
and father to Jonah

Damian,
Demon warrior

Mya,
Gordon and
Council Member

image COMICS
ILLUSTRATED QUALITY PAPER FULL BLEED COMIC PAGES
BOOK EPOCH
ISSUE# 1
PG# 3
ERIC
241
printed by BLUELINEPRO.COM

image COMICS
ILLUSTRATED QUALITY PAPER FULL BLEED COMIC PAGES
BOOK EPOCH
ISSUE# 1
PG# 6
ERIC/
stats
code
printed by BLUELINEPRO.COM

Coming Next from
Heroes and Villains Entertainment

SON OF MERLIN

Robert Napton • Zid

On the following pages,
Top Cow proudly presents
a special preview of Son of Merlin #1

CENTRAL PARK,
NEW YORK.

IN THIS DARKEST HOUR LET LIGHT STREAM FORTH INTO THE MINDS OF ALL HUMANITY...
ELEMENTS OF EARTH, WIND, WATER AND FIRE, BE WITH US THIS NIGHT...
"LET YOUR MAGIC EMPOWER OUR RITE."

OSCAILT!
OSCAILT AMACH!

LA FEY INDUSTRIES
LA FEY INDUSTRIES
LA FEY INDUSTRIES
LA FEY INDUSTRIES
SNIFF! SNIFF!
RRH?
SNIFF! SNIFF!
RUGH?

EIREABALL!

GWEN?
THERE YOU ARE.
WAS STARTING TO WONDER IF YOU WERE GOING TO LEAVE ME HERE.
LA FEY INDUSTRIES
WHY WOULD I DO THAT?
TEACH ME A LESSON ABOUT NOT RUNNING INTO SITUATIONS BY MYSELF TRYING TO IMPRESS YOU. ***THE USUAL.***
NICE SPELL. I'VE BEEN TRYING TO GET OUT OF THE CHAINS SINCE I WOKE UP HERE, BUT NONE OF MY TRICKS WORKED.

LET'S MOVE.
AFTER YOU.
LA FEY INDUSTRIES. SO SHE MUST BE AROUND.
SHE'S *HERE.*
WHAT IS IT?
SOMETHING JUST LATCHED ONTO ME.
GO RAIBH AMHLAAIDH.
UH, ENGLISH PLEASE.
A BINDING CIRCLE -- A VERY POWERFUL BINDING CIRCLE -- BLOCKING MUCH OF MY POWER.

The Top Cow essentials checklist:

Artifacts Volume 1
(ISBN: 978-1-60706-201-1)

Art of Top Cow Softcover
(ISBN: 978-1-60706-099-4)

Broken Trinity Volume 1
(ISBN: 978-1-60706-051-2)

The Darkness: Accursed Volume 1
(ISBN: 978-1-58240-958-0)

The Darkness: Origins Volume 1
(ISBN: 978-1-60706-097-0)

Artifacts Origins: First Born
(ISBN: 978-1-60706-506-7)

Freshmen Volume 1
(ISBN: 978-1-58240-593-3)

Magdalena Volume 1
(ISBN: 978-1-60706-206-6)

Rising Stars Volume 1
(ISBN: 978-1-58240-172-0)

Wanted
(ISBN: 978-1-58240-497-4)

Witchblade: Origins Volume 1
(ISBN: 978-1-58240-901-6)

Witchblade: Redemption Volume 1
(ISBN: 978-1-60706-193-9)

For more info , ISBN and ordering information on our latest collections go to:

www.topcow.com

Ask your retailer about our catalogue of our collected editions, digests and hard covers or check the listings at:

Barnes and Noble,
Amazon.com
and other fine retailers.

To find your nearest comic shop go to:

www.comicshoplocator.com